the
Winter
garden

Dedication
For my grandmother
Lucy, who introduced
me to gardening at the
age of three. And for my
mother Iris, who instilled
me with a sense fun
and enthusiasm about
everything.

Val Bourne

the Winter garden

Create a garden that
shines through the
forgotten season

CASSELL
ILLUSTRATED

contents

introduction

THE WINTER GARDEN can be as comforting as hot chocolate after a long winter walk because, as the days shorten and the temperatures plummet, there are some stunning changes in the garden. When many of our herbaceous plants take refuge underground, they leave space for crisply rich evergreens or other plants with winter presence to shine on an otherwise bare stage. These blocks of leaf sustain us through winter with all the potency of the Green Man. And when our deciduous shrubs and trees shed their leaves they reveal twiggy contours and fine tracery as delicate as Lalique crystal.

All this would go unnoticed in normal light, but in winter the sun sinks to its lowest point in the sky and pinpoints everything with a sharp clarity lacking at other times of the year. As it slants through bare branches it exaggerates every twist and turn, picks up textures on paths, trunks and buildings and deepens the winter palette of olive greens, tomato reds and faded browns, blacks and beiges. I see this stripping away as the gardening equivalent of the life laundry – less clutter and less summer froth define what your garden is about, or should be about, giving you the chance for some quiet reflection.

If you're lucky, frost descends too. It's the icing on the winter-gardening cake and if you've left late-season perennials and grasses in place, they will enchant you on a daily basis as they tremble and move with a faded decadence of their own. Or you may get grey, water-soaked mists that cling to cobwebs, soft layers of snow or sharply bright days with cobalt-blue skies. These colourful skies are so much more winning than the lavender-blue pallor of high summer and they provide a perfect backdrop for early blossom or flower. And many winter flowers, though insignificant in themselves, are highly fragranced. They're sirens looking to lure the earliest bee by drugging them with a sweet opiate – and we can fall under their spell too.

Most of us find ourselves housebound by shorter days and it gives us time to gaze over our gardens on lazy weekends from a warm window where we sit.

Or we rush up pathways to the door, key in hand, and planting winter gems in such places lifts our spirits when they flag on dark winter days.

Luckily we don't have to wait long to see signs of new life stirring. It may be a pink peony bud thrusting through the launch-pad soil with all the energy of a rocket, or a frilled sedum shoot defying the winter temperatures, pigeon-breast grey against barren-brown earth. Or it could be a glint of fresh-yellow star on a winter jasmine, or an early aconite bravely unfurling. That one tiny sign of the new gardening year will send the blood rushing and the old excitement and enthusiasm will bubble once again, stirring the pagan or druid deep in every gardener's soul.

Val Bourne 2006

texture
and
line

1

Once the garden retreats underground and the leaves head downwards, the main brushstrokes of the winter garden rely on woody plants; of these, small ornamental trees make the biggest impact on the eye. Always try and include at least one tree, for gardens devoid of trees somehow lack soul, particularly in winter.

texture and substance

Most modern gardens are small, and there may be room for three or four trees at most — sometimes only one — so it's vital to make careful choices in order to get the best varieties. A good tree, particularly if space is at a premium, should offer attractions for at least three seasons — ornamental bark or a striking habit in winter, blossom in spring, and fruits or colourful leaves in autumn, for example. An ill-chosen tree may offer little in the way of aesthetic charm and may shine in one season only, as is the case with the many frilled flowering cherries, or they may outgrow their space and look entirely out of kilter with the scale of the garden. Fast-growing trees have a tendency to be ungainly, like lanky adults. In either case, whether plain uninspiring or just too large in relation to the space available, the gardener will be forced to remove the costly mistake after five years or so, when the consequences of their ill-chosen choice can be ignored no longer. Removing trees is not only a difficult and energetic process, requiring real muscle, it is also heartbreaking. The tree fairy screams 'don't cut me down you vandal' every time it sees you weighing up the considerations of when, if and how. And, when the deed is done, even teetotallers like me feel in need of a large brandy to restore their gardening karma.

When selecting a choice tree, it makes good sense to seek expert guidance from a first-rate nursery, where someone can advise on the various options taking into account your locality, soil type and the kind of tree you're looking for. After all, tree planting isn't like dibbling in a perennial flower, which can be moved or ditched if troublesome. Trees are permanent and are likely to outlive you, and a well-chosen tree can give you years of pleasure.

The trees in this chapter are perfect for smaller gardens, as they grow slowly and reach a maximum height of 15m (50ft) when mature. If this sounds huge, please remember that most small trees take over 150 years to reach optimum height. Most gardeners when planting should consider the height the tree will reach after 20 years, which will, in many cases, eventually reach up to 5m (15ft).

RIGHT *The coppery spiders of the witch hazel* Hamamelis x intermedia *'Jelena' stand out against a background of ghost bramble (*Rubus biflorus*).*

PREVIOUS PAGES *The vivid orange stems of willows (*Salix alba var. vitellina *'Britzensis') threaded through white-stemmed Himalayan birches (*Betula utilis var. jacquemontii*) at Lady Farm in Somerset.*

All the trees in this chapter offer something magical in winter, whether it is striking bark, an attractive contour or a seductive shape, coloured stems, or warmly tipped buds. It's worth remembering that when winter descends the bark on most deciduous trees looks more animated than at other times of the year, because the light filters down at an angle through the bare branches and picks up the detail. The large plane trees (*Platanus orientalis*) grown along Japanese streets, for instance, seem strongly patched in overlapping splashes of cream, beige and pistachio-green; they're one of my lasting memories of a winter visit to Japan, and the bark struck me as being as significant as the earliest blossom. Nearer to home, the ridged bark of a mature oak (*Quercus robur*) bears a vertical pattern and is almost reptilian in texture; it tempts you to rub up against it and touch. But both of these enormous trees would be too vast for the average garden, and we're looking for small trees with winter sparkle. Having said that, if you admire a fine small to medium-sized tree, the bark is likely to have some attraction in winter even if it isn't in the Top 20 hit parade.

Birches

If you're considering an ornamental tree for winter interest, the birch is the strongest contender. Birches are airy, elegant trees, and most cast an attractive dappled light over the garden because of their well-spaced branches and twigs. They are extremely hardy and survive in exposed positions, and are very tolerant of a range of situations and soil types, including dry sites (they even thrive in my dry garden). All birches with coloured bark keep their attraction throughout the year – the bark just becomes more conspicuous and stunning as winter takes grip.

Birch bark is warmly tactile to the touch, and on a cold winter's day I have often sidled up to my Himalayan birch (*Betula utilis*) and felt its warmth and dry sheen on my fingertips. It's living reassurance that the garden still ticks away like a hibernating animal, resting but not dead. And if you've ever worn thickly textured silk, birch bark shares that same life-like texture. Pleasing to touch at any time, but sensational on a chilly day.

Another feature of birch bark is that it peels away in strips. This adds an extra dimension, because the underside of pale birch bark, which is revealed as the bark peels, is nearly always stronger in colour than the outside. It may be a warm cinnamon-tobacco-brown or a sparky paprika-spice red, for example, and looks very effective flapping against the whiter, paler exterior. As a child, I pulled off (though very gently I may add) strips of birch bark and composed poems on the lighter side of the papery skin. This was before the days of play centres and i-pods, and I know it makes me sound absurd, but if you visit any arboretum in autumn, you'll notice that small children continue to be drawn towards the flaking edges (admittedly, I haven't yet seen them thoughtfully jotting anything down!).

And then there are the lenticels, those horizontal raised bands that appear on the bark in a slightly darker tone – like braille messages from the tree spirit – and provide yet more texture. Many birches also have almost-black twiggy growth, and the combination of a pale trunk with that darkly fine tracery is an extremely striking combination in low winter light.

As well as having attractive bark, the foliage of most birches colours to mellow yellow in autumn, and the tight catkins add further winter interest.

Birches make fine single specimens set in a lawn. Alternatively, you could plant a small grove of three or five in a group together. When choosing a birch, it's worth considering multi-stemmed specimens, or planting three

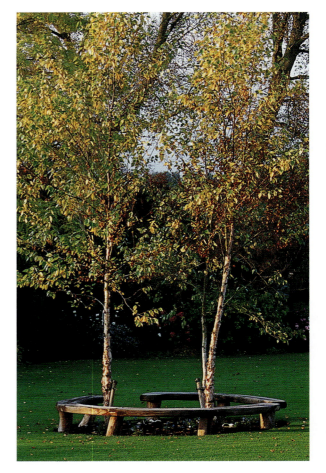

ABOVE *This simple curved bench encloses a cluster of* Betula nigra *'Heritage', enhancing their role as an ornamental feature.*

trees of the same variety in the same hole to create a multi-stemmed look. This avoids three or four sentry trees sticking up out of the garden, rather like lollipops.

SILVER SHADOWS The whitest trunk of all the birches belongs to the Himalayan birch (*Betula utilis*), but this tree has a range stretching from south-west China to Nepal and forms vary, particularly in size and stature. Also, not all forms of *Betula utilis* have white bark, and when you consider that the silver-white bark appears only after the tree has matured and reached its fifth year or more, it can be a lottery buying an unnamed form. Instead, I recommend you seek out a named variety from a respected tree nursery. White-barked forms of the Himalayan birch are often labelled *B. utilis* var. *jacquemontii* but, again, these trees vary in size and some grow very rapidly.

BELOW *This multi-stemmed form of* Betula ermanii *'Grayswood Hill', set among Himalayan birches (B. utilis), will gleam in winter light.*

If you have a small garden, the best named forms of *B. utilis* var. *jacquemontii* to look for are 'Silver Shadow', 'Jermyns' and 'Doorenbos'.

Of these, 'Silver Shadow' is the most desirable for small gardens because although the trunk is slower to whiten than the other two, taking about ten years to look its best, this form is slower-growing than the others and only reaches roughly 8m (25ft) when mature. The leaves of 'Silver Shadow' are larger than the species, a darker richer green, and the branches are slightly pendulous too, so there's good contrast between the foliage and the trunk for the rest of the year. The original 'Silver Shadow' came from Hillier's West Hill Nurseries near Winchester; it has reached 5m (15ft) in 11 years. You can also see this cultivar close to Weatherhill Cottage at Wisley.

My other recommendation, 'Jermyns', has a Hillier connection too. It bears the name of the late Sir Harold Hillier's house and garden in Jermyn's Lane, near Romsey in Hampshire. This garden, now called the Sir Harold Hillier Garden and Arboretum, opens to the public and is an inspirational garden to visit all year round. 'Jermyns' is larger in stature and faster-growing than 'Silver Shadow', reaching about 15m (50ft) when mature. The trunk starts to colour after three or four years in the ground, and by the time it is about seven years old it is a magnificent, dazzling white colour.

'Doorenbos' is also a fine silver birch. It has the added advantage of being the quickest of the three to produce that shimmering pale bark, taking just five years or so. The underside of the bark is pleasingly orange-cream too. 'Grayswood Ghost' is another good cultivar with larger leaves than the species.

LEFT *The peeling papery bark of Betula albosinensis – the Chinese red-bark birch – unfurls to reveal the warmly spiced trunk.*

RIGHT *The most tactile bark of all belongs to the aptly named paper-bark maple, Acer griseum.*

RICHER, WARMER BARK

Think of a white Himalayan birch trunk and then add a hint of brown-pink, the colour of cooked chestnut, and you have conjured up the delights of *Betula ermanii*, also known as Erman's birch. The bark of this native of north-east Asia and Japan is just as tactile as that of the white Himalayan birch, and the lenticels (those raised horizontal bumps) are more regularly distributed round the trunk and form a real feature of this tree. The leaves are larger and more pointed. Choose your tree carefully, as some forms of *B. ermanii* can reach about 18m (60ft) in height when mature. 'Grayswood Hill' is the finest form, with wonderful foliage.

The Chinese red-bark birch (*Betula albosinensis*) is a native of western China, and most have copper-red bark. However, an exceptional form, *B. albosinensis* var. *septentrionalis*, combines a pale creamy pink trunk with a spicy red underside. This choice tree reaches 14m (46ft) when mature. Another named form that is new to cultivation, 'Chinese Garden', has rich pink bark that exfoliates to reveal red bark underneath.

Some birches can provide you with golden bark in winter, although they are perhaps not quite as stunning as the silver-trunked varieties. The best of these, *Betula medwedewii* 'Gold Bark', is a small tree or large multi-stemmed shrub with butter-yellow foliage in autumn and upward-facing catkins throughout winter. *B. chinensis* 'Alberich's Gold' is another handsome

gold-barked birch tree, named and selected by
Bluebell Nursery and it has the advantage of
showing its golden bark after five years, whereas
B. medwedewii 'Gold Bark' usually takes ten.
You could also consider growing *B. lenta*, the
cherry bark birch, for its warm red to grey bark
and golden autumn tints.

UNDERPLANTING BIRCHES   Birches are
shallow-rooted and therefore many plants struggle
when grown close to their roots, so you need to
choose companion plants carefully. Pale birch
bark, whether surrounded by grass or seen against
bare earth, is a handsome feature in any garden in
winter. But in smaller gardens, you could enhance
the effect with a bright contrast. It could be warm-
stemmed, low-growing dogwoods (either *Cornus
sanguinea* 'Midwinter Fire' or the stronger, more
robust 'Midwinter Flame'), or the fiery red sacred bamboo, *Nandina domestica*,
which has pink-red leaves and can produce vibrant red fruits in warm locations.

ABOVE   *The autumn-flowering*
Cyclamen hederifolium *adds
the necessary spark of colour
between bare earth and the
creamy pink-tinted bark of*
Betula ermanii.

Low-growing evergreens, such as *Euonymus fortunei* 'Emerald 'n' Gold',
the glossy-green ground-cover ivy, *Hedera helix* 'Ivalace', with its delightfully
ruched leaves, or a small, blue-flowered periwinkle, for example *Vinca minor*
'La Grave', could also surround the tree. And many low-growing spring bulbs,
including the bright cobalt-blue *Scilla siberica*, would look dazzling against the
pale bark once spring arrives. The dappled, silver-spotted leaves of a choice
pulmonaria, such as *Pulmonaria* 'Trevi Fountain', would blend with the bark,
and in spring the bright blue flowers would add extra sparkle to the planting.

The best combination round a specimen birch grown in an open position
is a ring-planting of diminutive spring-flowering hardy cyclamen, *Cyclamen
coum*. The short, squat flowers are barely 8cm (3in) high and bright pink,
although there are white and blush-pink forms too; all forms have a magenta
"nose". These jaunty flowers can appear from midwinter onwards, creating a
clear contrast between the pale trunk and the bright flowers. The rounded
kidney-shaped leaves can be plain green or frosted silver and these appear
either with the flowers, or shortly afterwards. There is a period of summer
dormancy, when the leaves die back, but by then there will be other
distractions on the horizon – the garden will be in full swing. *C. coum* forms
small corms, roughly 3–5cm (1¼–2in) across; although the corms are short-
lived by nature, this species will obligingly self-seed round the birch trunk,
perpetuating the display. In summer, the cyclamen seeds are moved around
by ants, which lick off the sticky coat before discarding the seeds. New corms
will then appear. You could mulch with a layer of good bark chippings if you
like a tidy look.

Rich mahogany sheen

In addition to the birches, there are other trees with attractive winter bark, in stronger, warmer shades. The most well-known example with mahogany-coloured bark is *Prunus serrula,* commonly called the Tibetan cherry, although it also grows in China. This is a small, slow-growing tree, with a satin-gloss trunk that is heavily banded with large, duller lenticels. In winter, the sheen of the bark is highly attractive, and I know some gardeners who buff it up with a duster. Another reason this tree is so useful is that the wide crown and the twiggy branches of the willow-like leaves don't cast deep shade – always an advantage in a small garden. In spring, the small white flowers are abundant and pretty, rather than spectacular. This cherry is tolerant of all soils and situations, making it a strong candidate for every garden.

The rich shades of *Prunus serrula* mix very happily with pink-toned spring flowers, either plummy oriental hellebores (forms of *Helleborus* x *hybridus*) or 'China Pink' tulips. The tree also looks good underplanted with snowdrops or early daffodils, for example the short, bright yellow- and orange-cupped *Narcissus* 'Jetfire', or the pale yellow, rather willowy, wild-daffodil-lookalike 'W.P. Milner'.

BELOW *Prunus serrula has lovely high-gloss mahogany bark. It is a lightly canopied tree that can be used in mixed borders of shrubs and perennials.*

Both the snowdrops and the daffodils could provide the necessary break between the dark soil and trunk. I think it needs this buffer zone, to highlight the deep patina of the bark, which doesn't show up against winter earth.

Papery cinnamon

Two plants with interesting brown bark, the strawberry tree (*Arbutus*) and Persian ironwood (*Parrotia persica*), hover between being shrubs and small trees. Both make a contribution to the winter garden. The strawberry tree has evergreen leaves, scented white flowers and small, strawberry-like fruits. Some kinds have warm-brown, peeling bark. However, the commonest, *Arbutus unedo*, does not. Instead, you will need to seek out *A. andrachne*, the Greek strawberry tree, often called the madrona, which has rufous-orange, peeling bark that curls back to reveal the lighter wood beneath. Unfortunately, the Greek provenance of this tree means that it is tender, and most of us will struggle to keep it. The hybrid between the two, *A.* x *andrachnoides*, is hardier and more vigorous, and therefore a safer choice. Strawberry trees are often mis-named by nurseries (some advertise *A. unedo* as having wonderful peeling bark), so this can cause complications when selecting your tree; check the bark carefully before you buy.

Parrotia persica, the Persian ironwood, is more renowned for its red autumn tints, but once the leaves drop on mature specimens the bark also peels attractively. Parrotias need deep, fertile soil and plenty of space, being almost wider than they are tall, so they are not ideal for smaller gardens. Not every *P. persica* colours up well so, again, it is desirable to seek out a named form. 'Jodrell Bank' and 'Vanessa' both offer good autumn colour.

Several acers make fine winter specimens and have attractive papery or textured bark. Many are slow-growing, compact, and create interesting shapes: some have splayed-out branches when young, others form immaculate, neat, almost bonsai-like structures. Small ornamental acers need a sheltered site, protected from harsh frosts and strong winds. If given that advantage, many will shine.

Acer griseum, known as the paper-bark maple, is a small, slow-growing tree from China, reaching 10m (30ft) at most. The peeling bark is highly desirable, and this tree is obligingly quick to shed its bark on both its trunk and branches, revealing the brighter, cinnamon-coloured wood beneath. The three-lobed leaves, typical of most acers, will turn a bonfire-scarlet-red every autumn.

Snake-bark markings

Some ornamental acers display snake-bark markings on both the trunk and the branches; these markings deepen with the first frost of winter. Often, the striated marks are paler than their background colour and many combine a grey-green background colour with almost silver vertical ribboning. The trees look as though they have been colour-washed by a modern paint stylist. The bloom will even come off on your fingers, as if the painter is still at his art.

RIGHT *Many acers have linear striations on their bark, especially when young. Acer grosseri var. hersii is one of the finest.*

Acer grosseri var. *hersii* is a native of China, and is one of the finest small acers with smoothly ribboned bark. The branches are upright and form an interesting splayed shape. The overall colour of the wood is olive-green, and matches the leaves for most of the year. However, in autumn the foliage mellows to deep yellow, setting up a fine contrast against the green wood. In addition, the winged fruits are attractively large, at least 5cm (2in) across, and the tree reaches only about 10m (30ft) when mature, perhaps slightly larger in some conditions.

The Manchurian snake-bark maple, *Acer tegmentosum*, displays green bark, but with just a hint of cool oriental jade, overlaid with vertical silver striations. The mahogany buds in winter are another bonus. Unfortunately, this tree is hard to find. More commonly available, and with a similarly coloured trunk, is the snake-bark maple, *A. davidii,* from central China. Two named forms will give you a maroon and silver combination, rather than the usual green and silver. 'George Forrest' has almost purple bark when young, again with silver striations; 'Serpentine' has a silver-maroon bark striated in silver. Of the two, 'Serpentine' is probably more striking. Both are more heavily striated as young trees.

Many Asian plants have a similar equivalent found in North America. This dates back to when these massive continents were joined together, before

continental drift placed oceans between them. The North American equivalent of the Chinese *Acer davidii* is *A. pensylvanicum*, a tree with that same combination of jade-green bark overlaid with silver vertical bands. One form, *A. pensylvanicum* 'Erythrocladum', produces bright pink young growth in a strident shade that the late Barbara Cartland would have been proud to wear. All forms of *A. pensylvanicum* refuse to grow on chalk, however, and there's always an element of 'will it or won't it thrive' with this rather miffy tree.

The hybrid between the American snake-bark maple (*Acer pensylvanicum*) and the Chinese snake-bark maple (*A. davidii*) is called *A.* x *conspicuum*, and some of the named forms of this hybrid also have vivid pink markings on the trunk and branches. The colour becomes more intense with the first frost of the year. *A.* x *conspicuum* 'Phoenix' is described by Robert Vernon (of the Bluebell Arboretum at Ashby de la Zouch) as having branches the colour of Patsy's lipstick (this will only mean something to aficionados of Joanna Lumley and *Absolutely Fabulous*). The bark mellows back to a cool green when winter is over. 'Silver Cardinal' is a cream- and pink-variegated form with bark striated in silver.

These snake-bark maples all form small trees, of almost shrub size, and need their own space if they're to be seen to full effect in winter. However, all acers thrive under a canopy of larger trees, and this setting protects them from late frost, which can scorch off the emerging foliage and actually kill young trees. When buying acers, I feel it's worth spending the maximum amount for a more mature tree, as older specimens can shrug off frost much better than younger ones.

For a different effect of overlapping mottled colours, varying between cream, brown, charcoal and grey, consider the lace-bark pine, *Pinus bungeana*, from northern China. Although this can reach up to 30m (100ft) in China, Britain and many other places it rarely reaches 3m (10ft). The branching habit and dark, shiny pine needles held in groups of three make this an interesting specimen tree.

Eucalypts often have patchwork bark too, but I cannot recommend them as they grow very quickly and tend to be short-lived. They're just too fast out of the blocks, and that glaucous foliage and leaning habit seem to jar against the European landscape.

BELOW Pinus bungeana, *the lace-bark pine.*

Choosing a tree

GENERALLY, WHICHEVER VARIETY OF TREE YOU choose, you should buy a small, young specimen, because in most cases they suffer less stress when transplanted (acers are an exception). Although they may look like slender whips, they will soon catch up with the larger, highly expensive specimens you see winched into show gardens. For every time a large mature tree is bought and planted, there's a high risk that it will simply go backwards before turning up its toes. Young trees, like young people, are adaptable beings, raring to get going. Take advantage of their keenness and, like spotty teenagers at the beginning of adolescence, they will soon blossom and flourish.

Bare-root or container-grown?

Once you have visited an arboretum or two (preferably in all four seasons) and have made your choice of tree based on advice given, the next decision involves choosing between a bare-root tree, which needs planting during the dormant season (between late autumn and early spring), or a container-grown specimen, which can be planted almost any time, provided the weather is not too hot or too cold.

Bare-root trees have several advantages. They tend to be less expensive and smaller, they can often be ordered by mail order and, once planted, they usually romp away. But increasingly, many nurseries that specialise in choice trees sell container-grown specimens only, in order to satisfy the year-round demand from customers. These container specimens can be collected and planted at any time of the year.

Some nurseries lift entire trees and shrubs, wrapping the rootball in hessian. If your nursery performs this task while you wait, before your very eyes, and you can rush home and plant it, that's fine. Otherwise, don't invest in something that could have dried-out roots.

Spring or autumn planting?

My advice on planting container-grown trees is to try and capitalise on one of the two main growth spurts if you can, planting either in early autumn or in spring. Both times have their advantages and disadvantages.

Spring-planted specimens may well encounter a severe spring drought and cold easterly winds in mid- and late spring. They will always need regular watering for their first six months. Autumn-planted specimens can romp away early in the season, when the soil is warm and moist, but then they may encounter winter storms and harsh weather within their first winter. There is no need to water them in autumn.

Soil and situation may dictate your timing. If you have a heavy, clay soil, the general rule is to plant in spring, once the soil has begun to dry out and warm up. Cold, claggy soil round a rootball kills more plants in their first six months than anything else (ask yourself whether you would survive a long cold bath in winter!). It's vital to make a planting hole considerably larger than the rootball of your tree to allow for the addition of some bulky organic matter. This will improve drainage around the tree's roots and prevent the hole filling with water. Mulch every year with organic matter, either in early autumn or early spring. Lighter, well-drained soils inevitably dry out more severely in spring if there hasn't been much rain, so where this is the case, autumn planting is preferable. If you plant in autumn, you don't need to water and mulching is best left until the following spring.

The key test when evaluating your soil type is to take a small handful and mould it together after heavy rain. Light, friable soil refuses to form a tight ball and therefore maintains its open structure, even in wet winters. Heavy soil, which usually has a clay content, will have the texture of Plasticine when rolled in the hand and will form a small shiny ball, reducing in size as you press. It will even show your fingerprints if the clay content is high. This type of clay soil is easily compacted by feet when wet, and you must always work off wooden planks when treading on wet clay to avoid compacting

the surface. Having said that, clay soil is highly fertile and many woody plants positively thrive on it.

Having defined your soil type, examine your aspect and situation. Gardens on the western half of Britain, for example, are often clemently warm in winter and the climate is usually soft enough to encourage a newly planted tree through its first winter. Compare that with one of my previous gardens, set high in the Northamptonshire wolds. It was blasted by arctic winds from the Russian Urals for much of every year and temperatures plummeted to −32°C (−26°F) in severe winters. Under these conditions, spring planting was the only option, both for the gardener and for the plant.

Whatever your soil and situation, remember the golden rule is to avoid planting anything in extremely cold or extremely hot weather.

Good planting

Planting trees is hard work, but good preparation pays dividends and your tree will grow away quickly. I've learnt through experience that planting things well, in effect giving them a banquet on arrival, ensures a plant's wellbeing for years to come. If you scrimp now, your tree is likely to sulk for at least two or three years.

Dig a large hole, at least twice the size of the rootball. Add well-rotted organic matter from a compost heap. I do not recommend animal manure, as this can scorch new tree roots. If garden compost isn't available, invest in four or five large bags of soil-based John Innes mixture No. 3 and add that to the hole instead. Don't use peat; if it dries out you can't rehydrate it, and nothing kills a plant more effectively than a dry peat ball round the roots.

Before planting, very gently tease out any roots that resemble the circle line on the tube map and splay them downwards. Place the tree so that the rootball is level with the soil (if the tree is grafted, leave the graft uncovered), and backfill with soil and organic matter if you wish. Gently firm the soil with your feet and water well. Always add a stake and a tree tie when you plant, to stop the tree rocking in the wind. The stake can be removed after two or three years, but remember to check the tightness of the tree tie every few months – if it cuts into the bark, the tree will die. Also, use a circular mulch mat, because newly planted trees need as little competition as possible. The mulch mat will smother weeds and conserve moisture in one go.

Once you have selected a tree or two for the texture and substance they bring to the winter garden, you may like to consider some of the shrubs, trees and bamboos with coloured stems in winter.

colourful stems

Space may well dictate and restrict your choices, but many of the plants with coloured stems can be accommodated in containers by doorways. Whether you grow them in a container or in the ground, the sun has to strike the bare stems if they are to shine. You can't hide these away in deep shade if you're growing them for winter colour.

Dogwoods

The straight-stemmed dogwoods (*Cornus*) are easy and accommodating, and provide olive-green, greenish yellow, almost black or red stems. Their best colour is produced on one-year-old wood. All the straight-stemmed dogwoods should be radically pruned every year. There are two methods. Either you can remove the dullest stems at ground level every spring. This encourages new growth, but the shrub still has some presence. Alternatively, if yearly pruning seems too onerous, you can remove every stem at ground level in spring every other year. Whichever method you choose, when you've removed the stems, water the shrub well and give it an organic feed. The powdery 6X fertiliser is easy to apply and handle. I think yearly pruning gives the best results.

The reddest stems of all belong to a form of the red-barked dogwood, *Cornus alba* 'Sibirica', a plant often sold and labelled 'Westonbirt'. This has plain green leaves that turn a damson red before they drop in mid-autumn, to reveal bright scarlet stems. However, owners of small gardens may prefer to grow other forms with more interesting foliage. There is a variegated cream and green

LEFT *The red stems of Cornus alba 'Sibirica' dramatised by snow.*

ABOVE *Colourful stems are enhanced by still water – they allow a Monet-like reflection. At Lady Farm in Somerset, willows and birches are echoed by bullrushes at the water's edge.*

form of 'Sibirica', although it is said to be less vigorous. 'Aurea' has yellow leaves early in the year, though these dull to green as summer wears on. 'Spaethii' has leaves with golden variegation and these are good for adding light and shade or illuminating a dank corner. My preferred variety, 'Elegantissima', has light green leaves mottled in cream; the foliage contrasts well with the red stems and they look attractive during spring and summer.

All these red-barked dogwoods grow naturally between Siberia and Manchuria and also in North Korea. They are very hardy and tolerate all soils and conditions. Their greatest attribute is that they are able to thrive in damp soils, which makes them useful close to water, either beside still ponds or running streams. The reflections of the stems in the water are an added bonus.

There are also Russian red-stemmed varieties (*Cornus alba*) and North American dogwoods with olive to ochre stems, called *C. sericea* (formerly *C. stolonifera*) 'Flaviramea'. Both kinds can be used successfully in winter containers as well as borders. They mix well in containers grown with ivies and green-leaved skimmias, for instance. A dark-stemmed form, called *Cornus alba* 'Kesselringii', has purplish black stems, which provide striking verticals in a white winter landscape.

Multi-stemmed, twiggy dogwoods provide an alternative to the straight-stemmed varieties, but they need a much more gentle pruning regime. All that is required is a gentle tidy in spring, so you must separate them from the straight-stemmed dogwoods in your mind, before you get secateur-happy. If you cut these twiggier dogwoods back too vigorously they are likely to disappear forever. Their fine stems waver between red and orange in colour. The most well-known form, *Cornus sanguinea* 'Winter Beauty', is a flickering mixture of colours. *C. sanguinea*, known as common dogwood, is native to much of Europe, including Britain, but I can see little common ground between this vigorous native dogwood, found in country hedges by the yard, and the round, twiggy bush selected in Holland. The leaves on the wild forms go damson red, but 'Winter Beauty' and 'Midwinter Flame', another more robust and vigorous selection, turn orange-yellow as winter approaches.

Confusingly, there are also flowering dogwoods grown for their large, petal-like bracts; they are lovely, but they are more demanding in terms of their soil requirements and they offer no particular winter beauty of their own.

When planting winter-stemmed dogwoods, you can either have one specimen bush or group three or five together in a triangular drift. Always avoid straight lines and lollipop clusters; instead, drift your plants in long ribbons wherever possible. Wherever winter-stemmed dogwoods are grown in a garden, setting up a contrast with evergreen low-growing plants is a good idea. The hardy ferns, principally polystichums and polypodiums, have excellent vibrant green winter fronds that combine beautifully with dogwoods, particularly the red-stemmed ones.

Acers and willows

Some acers provide more than just beautifully coloured leaves, or textured bark, they also have dramatically coloured stems. Pruning the stems back to the trunk in spring will create a flush of new growth that will ensure winter excitement. One species that responds particularly well to this is *Acer negundo*, a fast-growing American acer commonly called box elder. A new form, called 'Winter Lightning', produces gleaming, golden, shiny stems when cut back hard. You can also hard-prune the violet-branched form, *A. negundo* var. *violaceum*, but you may prefer to leave it and enjoy the hanging tassels of reddish pink flowers in spring.

LEFT *Orange-red is the warmest winter colour and the young stems of Salix alba var. vitellina 'Britzensis' – the scarlet willow – can be used as a single specimen.*

RIGHT *The striking greenish yellow stems of Cornus sericea 'Flaviramea' shine in winter light; grow it in full sun for best effect. It provides good contrast with red-stemmed varieties or evergreen shrubs.*

Several willows are useful for their colourful stems, and these can be pruned back to the trunk every spring to promote that bright young growth. But do remember willows need moisture. They also tend to be larger than dogwoods. The most commonly grown, *Salix alba* var. *vitellina* 'Britzensis', also known as the scarlet willow, is normally pruned back to the trunk to produce an orange haze of young stems. Another form, *S. alba* 'Hutchinson's Yellow', if pruned in the same way, will give you golden yellow stems.

The violet willow, *Salix daphnoides,* is really a fast-growing tree, but it can be pruned back hard every spring to give fresh, dusky stems each winter. And these stems have a paler bloom. 'Aglaia', a male form, will give you handsome fluffy buds and catkins too.

But perhaps the most stunning willow of all, as far as catkins are concerned, is *Salix gracilistyla* 'Melanostachys'. This shrubby plant produces stunning black catkins with red anthers. Because the catkins are best on more mature wood, you need to thin out the stems of this willow rather than cut them all back.

Ghost brambles

Most of the coloured stems mentioned up to this point make a strong vertical shape in the garden, but another group of plants, the ghost brambles (*Rubus*), tend to have arching branches. The ghost brambles are beautiful to gaze upon. Their silvery stems often have a damson bloom and, seen against a winter sun, seem like an ice-bound fountain stretching up to heaven before cascading downward. But gardeners who know their Latin will immediately associate the name *Rubus* with the blackberry, and then a nanosecond later the word 'prickly' will appear on their consciousness. They are severely prickly – as with a teenager with their first hangover, approach with caution. Ghost brambles need to be in an area of the garden where you aren't going to rip open your gardening coat or your knuckles as you pass. They are also difficult to establish, well, they have been in my garden at any rate – they seem to take a year or so to make up their minds.

The most thuggish, and therefore the most dramatic ice-fountain of all is *Rubus cockburnianus*, a thick-stemmed Chinese bramble with stems bloomed in damson and silver. The ferny, finely divided leaves also have a white bloom on their undersides, and these make a strong summer feature too. There is a golden-leaved form called 'Goldenvale', which is less aggressive in growth and has whiter stems. *R. thibetanus* 'Silver Fern', another bramble, has stems with a blue-white bloom and greyish leaves. These curving stems, softly bloomed, will look handsome in winter and can be enhanced by a surrounding ring of the low-growing, black-leaved grass *Ophiopogon planiscapus* 'Nigrescens'.

LEFT The black strappy leaves of Ophiopogon planiscapus 'Nigrescens' *make a contrasting carpet for the silver fountains of* Rubus thibetanus 'Silver Fern'.

Fiery spindles

Euonymus (or spindles) are accommodating shrubs or trees that tolerate most sites, even dryish shade. All the deciduous species have fiery red foliage in early autumn, and the shoots of some varieties give good winter value; some stems have pale brown stripes against a darker background, while others have corky wings. Many also bear winged fruits, a day-glo concoction of vivid orange-red and strident pink, from early autumn onwards. My own personal favourite is *Euonymus planipes*, a branching spindle that bears a good number of large fruits in early autumn, although these have always gone by late autumn. However, *E. europaeus* 'Red Cascade' is smothered in many red fruits that persist into winter, as is *E. alatus*. The latter has the added attraction of branches edged in corky wings.

Colour-tipped buds

Some trees produce colourful buds, for example *Tilia cordata* 'Winter Orange', a new small-leaved lime tree, recently introduced to the UK. It has much better golden-orange young stems and buds in winter than the species and the glossy, heart-shaped leaves turn yellow in autumn. The flowers, which appear in midsummer, are sweetly scented too.

Bamboos

The shiny canes of bamboos can also come alive in winter light, and there are black-, golden and green-caned varieties on offer. Most are plain and come in one colour, which deepens in winter, but there are also vertically striped and mottled kinds. Most bamboos have ramrod-straight stems, but some are knuckled and contorted at the nodes, or even zigzag. These plant sculptures are highly tactile and attractive, and there is growing interest in them among modern gardeners who like simpler planting.

Growth rates of bamboos vary according to type and species, as well as climate. The key to growing bamboo is to seek expert help with your choices, so that you can grow the right variety for your garden, taking into account the space available. If you've ever tried to remove a large bamboo, you'll know it's a gardening nightmare! It is not a sensible option to grow bamboo in a container. It works in the short-term, but bamboos prefer to be grown in the ground as they show their distress quickly when lacking water and don't always recover.

Phyllostachys nigra is the most popular ornamental bamboo and the only black-caned bamboo on offer, although there are named forms. The canes start dark green and then mature to matt black after a season or two, and that's when the pale sheaf scar and the whitish narrow ring underneath the node really stand out against the dark cane. The average height is 6m (20ft) and the spread after ten years is 2.5–5m (8–15ft). 'Boryana' has canes marked in large blotches of dark brown or purplish black and, as they age, the green background fades to golden olive-yellow, showing the markings to full effect. 'Boryana' is more variable in habit than *P. nigra*. Its height after ten years can top 15m (50ft) with a spread of 1 to 4m (3 to 13ft) depending on soil conditions, fertility and climate.

Another bamboo, *Thamnocalamus crassinodus* 'Merlyn', forms a tall vertical collection of canes, and all new canes have a powder-blue bloom. It can reach 5m (15ft) with an average spread of 1.5m (15ft). The named form 'Kew Beauty' is quick to mature.

Of the seven golden-caned bamboos the most diminutive is *Phyllostachys aurea* 'Koi'. The stiff culms mature to a golden butter-yellow, but there are green internodal grooves running down the canes and irregular swellings close to some nodes. 'Koi' is compact, spreading to only 1.5m (5ft) after ten years and reaching a height of about 4m (13ft). It will catch the light, giving a glowing colour and texture.

LEFT *The golden stems of* Phyllostachys aureosulcata *enhanced by rich-green leaves.*

RIGHT *The black-stemmed* Phyllostachys nigra *takes two or three seasons to develop a matt-black finish.*

There is also a golden crook-stemmed bamboo called *Phyllostachys aureosulcata* f. *aureocaulis,* which benefits from a tidy habit and hardy constitution. Averaging 5m (15ft) in height and forming a clump no larger than 3m (10ft) wide after ten years, this shouldn't pose too much of a threat to the gardener. When winter sun catches the stems, the sunny sides take on an orange-red bloom, and this is the nearest to a red-stemmed bamboo you can find. The zigzagging stems are splayed out, but are not as severely kinked as the true species, *P. aureosulcata,* or the all-green Pekinese form (f. *pekinensis*).

Owners of large gardens might want to cultivate a large stunning bamboo, *Phyllostachys vivax* f. *aureocaulis.* The green striping on its golden stems is random, like a bar code, and when winter sun slants through the canes this tall bamboo, which can reach 8m (26ft), looks stunning. In early summer, when the plant is at its most active, you can almost see the stems heading skywards as you watch.

Most trees have fine tracery in winter, when viewed against a clear sky, but some trees have contorted stems twisted into corkscrew curls. The most well-known is the hazel, *Corylus avellana* 'Contorta'.

twists and turns

More shrub than tree, *Corylus avellana* 'Contorta' forms a low, rounded bush on a short trunk. In winter, you can enjoy all those intricate twists and turns decorated with tightly formed catkins; I also love the way the raindrops gather in every crinkle and turn. However, when summer arrives, leaves appear from every angle of the stems and the contorted hazel looks scruffier by the day. Some people prune it, leaving just a few long stems to glimmer and gleam in winter sun, but far better to put up with its raggedy summer clothing and enjoy the full glory of its habit in winter.

There is also a contorted willow, *Salix babylonica* var. *pekinensis* 'Tortuosa', commonly called the dragon's-claw willow, which forms an upright columnar tree with spiralling branches. Like all willows, it prefers moist soil and this fast-growing tree will suck out gallons of water from the soil and may stress other plants close by. Think carefully before you opt for this tree, unless you have lots of room and a high water table.

On a completely different scale, the corokia, a small shrub with forked stems, can also add interest, whether planted in well-drained soil or grown in a container. These New Zealand shrubs have specially adapted foliage which is unpalatable to grazing animals and can withstand windswept conditions. They have an intricate structure of metallic, grey stems dotted with spoon-shaped tiny leaves, usually equally metallic in tone. The undersides are often felted green and together stems and

BELOW *The corokia provides an intricate tracery of silvery branches dotted with the tiniest of leaves.*

leaves form a delicate network. All corokias are excellent in exposed positions, including close to the coast. They can even produce flowers and fruit in optimum conditions. *Corokia cotoneaster* is compact and commonly called the wire-netting bush, due to its gun-metal-grey tangle of stems studded with tiny leaves. These leaves are shiny on top and have felted undersides that provide an interesting texture. *C. x virgata* is a larger shrub with larger narrow leaves, although these still only measure 1cm (½in) in length.

All corokias need well-drained, friable soil to be grown in the ground, and gardeners who have heavy, cold soil or garden in areas with high rainfall will find them impossible to overwinter. However, corokias make excellent container plants in two respects – they are drought tolerant, thriving on summer neglect, and they are extremely slow-growing.

In winter, these intricate plant sculptures take on a new definition. Underplanting them with tiny species crocus, for example the pallid *Crocus chrysanthus* 'Cream Beauty', adds to the interest.

catching the frost

2

Frosts used to be a common occurrence – cutting through the garden in autumn, with the precision of a knife portioning out the summer and winter halves of a sponge cake. Nowadays, frosts are later and less frequent, often not occurring until after Christmas. When they finally arrive, the effects are quite magical, and their relative scarcity makes the pleasure they bring all the more intense.

silhouettes and tracery

Frost and ice cast a silvery presence, picking up fine detail, beading grasses, lining fine strands of faded umbellifer flowers, and catching the frilled and quilled edges of holly and ivy. They also add definition to inanimate objects – a tiled roof, a glazed summerhouse, and even a garden shed can take on all the interest of a textured tapestry when every curve and line is rimed in white-edged ice.

The sudden plunge in winter temperatures inevitably calls a sharp halt to growth in the garden. Tender plants – such as dahlias and salvias – blackened by the slightest plunge below zero, soon collapse and fade; herbaceous plants retreat underground, sometimes leaving strong vertical stems topped with fading flowers; leaves colour and drop, and the grass hugs the ground. As a result of all this, the garden seems to stretch larger and wider. The effect is the same when you drive through a winter landscape of bare fields, hedges and trees. The turreted church, which has been hidden in woodland for most of the year, or the distant villages in the fold of the hill far away, suddenly stand out more; the uncluttered view is clearer and sharper, and the world looks a larger place. In our gardens, we can capitalise on this illusion by creating a clear contrast between our tidied-up areas and pockets of planting, hard landscape, and specimen plants.

RIGHT *The upright stems of tall asters, southernwood (Artemisia abrotanum) and Phlomis russeliana make a brilliant contrast with the sheath of leaves formed by Miscanthus sinensis 'Gracillimus'.*

LEFT *West Green House in Hampshire uses texture and silhouette splendidly with solid, round box balls among bare trees. The focal point is a latticed gazebo.*

PREVIOUS PAGES *Late-season grasses and late-season perennials often provide the finest silhouettes. Here, at Lady Farm, in Somerset, the upright stems of Calamagrostis x acutiflora 'Karl Foerster' head upwards like rockets. The feathery, gossamer awns of Miscanthus sinensis 'Silberfeder' soften the effect.*

Leaving some seedheads intact on the plants in your garden will help to create definition and will provide pleasure when frost descends. After all, if you insist on cutting everything down and flattening your garden to a bare expanse of earth, all the while congratulating yourself on having 'put the garden to bed early' (a phrase that makes my heart sink), you will never be able to enjoy the intricate spokes of a frosted fennel head or the delicacy of lace-paper hydrangea flowers, each bent down to form a pixie's rara skirt. In addition, cutting everything back will create a hostile wasteland for hibernating insects, bees, birds and small animals. Having said all this, I do have to agree that you can't leave a whole garden intact through the winter. Imagine the panic when spring breaks through, and everything needs a thorough tidy all at once.

Autumn clearance or healthy neglect?

For practicality's sake, you need to segregate your garden into those parts that need to be tidied in autumn and those that can, or should, be left until spring. Areas of the garden that are to shine in spring need overhauling in autumn, particularly places where there are spring bulbs growing – these must be cleared while the bulbs are still dormant, under a thick layer of earth, before they emerge or flower. Most early-season perennials (for example delphiniums, campanulas and lupins) also need cutting back; they shouldn't be left to produce seedheads, because their brown colour looks incongruous in the full flow of high summer. Also, soggy, floppy stems and flowerheads and soft, sappy rhubarb stems simply can't be left, as they look extremely messy over winter.

Generally, there are three types of plant that tend to have good winter seedheads or profiles, and should therefore be left alone in autumn to give pleasure in winter. The first group that provide good winter silhouettes are

BELOW Phlomis tuberosa 'Amazone' is one of the finest perennial phlomis, dying down and leaving a series of straight stems studded with chambered heads.

plants that endure warmer, wetter winters, such as most Mediterranean plants, some South African plants and some New Zealanders. Most Mediterranean plants are aromatic sun-lovers, and they include lavenders, phlomis, artemisias and cistus. They tend to be woody and stiff-stemmed throughout winter, and thrive in dry, well-drained, open, sunny sites. To generalise, most South African and New Zealand plants that give winter presence need sharp drainage, good light and a dry summer bake. However, many also like a burst of moisture too.

The second and third groups are the late-season perennials and grasses. Many of these do not flower until late summer, early autumn or mid-autumn, and they still have the ability to endure and make some winter impact. However, you cannot generalise and say that all late-season performers make great winter silhouettes. Soft-stemmed flowers, such as *Persicaria amplexicaulis* 'Firetail', flop to a soggy mess at the first sign of frost, so they are best cut down before you have to scrape them off the path. Others that seed prolifically – for example biennial foxgloves (*Digitalis purpurea*), teasels, biennial *Eryngium giganteum*, most tall, summer-flowering alliums and aquilegias – have to be culled at the 'rattling' stage because they produce an overwhelming number of seedlings.

RIGHT *The scented white flowers of bugbane* (Actaea simplex), *are borne on tall, slender stems – and they fade beautifully.*

Sun-loving plants that thrive in open, well-drained borders produce considerably better seedheads than plants that are grown in shade. This is because most shade-lovers are early into flower and they tend to be low-growing, so don't have the same impact and presence as the taller, sun-loving plants. Also, when they are in shade they don't catch the frost and glimmer in the same way as plants grown in the open. *Actaea simplex* (formerly *Cimicifuga simplex*) is an exception, as it is a moisture-loving plant that thrives in shade, and produces a series of upright, narrow, slender spikes with greenish white then brown, star-shaped seed-heads in winter.

When growing plants for winter interest, remember that it is stiff stems with a high wood content that persist into winter. Don't whack lots of nitrogen-rich fertiliser on the borders during summer, as this will promote lots of soft, fast, leafy growth. Instead, grow your plants in open, airy borders to allow them to develop strong, woody growth. In winter, when frost catches the remains of that billowing late-summer border, and the sun glints through it, you'll get maximum enjoyment.

Vestiges of the summer and autumn

Sun-loving Mediterranean aromatics, which shine in summer and require a sunny, well-drained border, tend to provide winter interest in the form of upright stems, bushy habit or attractive seedheads. The plants are on view all winter, because you leave them intact right up until late spring (once danger of frost has passed), when you cut them back to promote good, strong growth; if cut back in autumn, the new growth appearing at the base would almost certainly be killed by frost. Lavenders with tufted petals are an exception, as they need to be cut back after their first flush of flower in early summer.

SAGE-SCENTED PHLOMIS   One of the best Mediterranean sun-lovers you can grow, both for foliage and the seedheads, is the sage-scented phlomis. I grow many in dry, sunny sites in my garden. It's useful to subdivide them into those that are shrubby and those that are perennial. Shrubby phlomis keep their leaves throughout winter and stay above the ground, usually gaining height as they mature. Perennial phlomis retreat underground in bad weather,

although in mild winters they can and do stay in leaf. They are ground-hugging and spread in width rather than height. Despite being labelled perennial, these phlomis send up flowering stems that may reach 1.2m (4ft) in height, and they can make as much impact on the garden in summer as the shrubby phlomis.

All phlomis, including the herbaceous ones, have enduring seedheads that keep their shape through winter. These seedheads shelter many tiny insects both in their leaves, which are very effective ladybird blankets, and in the individual chambers within the seedhead. My collection of phlomis heads on the desk, freshly collected from the garden, has produced four seven-spot ladybirds and a couple of small spiders already. I have now released them back into the wild.

Shrubby phlomis can be damaged by frosts in late spring, and they may lose their leaves and flower buds. However, I have never lost a phlomis completely; they have all recovered. The most widely grown is *Phlomis fruticosa*, commonly called the Jerusalem sage. The whorled, hard yellow flowers are held on short stems and appear all over this grey-green-leaved evergreen shrub in mid-summer. The seedheads are very sturdy and can be left on the plant until spring, when they are best removed to expose the new flowers. Jerusalem sage

LEFT   *The multi-branched heads of all umbellifers persist into winter. Here,* Angelica sylvestris *'Vicar's Mead' supports a spirally cobweb.*

has an upright habit, and can reach over 2m (6ft), but it responds well to pruning after flowering if you want to restrict its size or legginess. Large, rangy specimens can be cut back hard, but it is best to do this in two or three stages, allowing one half to rejuvenate before tackling the other half. This shrub could be grown against a sunny wall, along a sunny path, or in the centre of an aromatic, sunny border.

Phlomis italica is a much daintier plant in every way. The long arrowhead leaves are woolly and silvered with white felt, and the small flowerheads produce dainty roundels of lilac-pink flowers in midsummer. I have always tucked this small, columnar evergreen shrub close to a sunny wall. The seedheads are not so much of a feature, being small, but this plant has a tight, neat habit and the white-felted leaves are stunning in winter light.

Further along the sunniest side of my house I grow another evergreen phlomis, with golden yellow flowers, called *Phlomis longifolia*. This is a fairly upright shrub, reaching about 1–1.2m (3–4ft), with relatively soft growth. The upper green surfaces of the arrowhead leaves (which are identical in shape to the foliage of *P. italica*) are heavily crinkled and textured, reminiscent of corded upholstery fabric. The undersides are a paler sage green, and the square stems (always a feature of phlomis and the labiate family in general) usually have a double whorl of lipped flowers, although some stems only bear one, others three; as the buds begin to break they are flecked in black. When the roundly neat seedhead appears it is tightly bound by sepals and measures 4cm (1½in) across.

Phlomis 'Edward Bowles' (raised by Hilliers in 1967) is a fine evergreen phlomis, with two-tone cream and pale yellow flowers and heart-shaped green leaves. However, it is difficult to place this firmly in either the shrubby or perennial sections because it is thought to be a hybrid between the shrubby *P. fruticosa* and the perennial *P. russeliana*. It stays above ground in most winters but follows the perennial growth habit of *P. russeliana*, spreading across the ground, although not as vigorously. 'Edward Bowles' can have four whorls of flower per stem and is the best summer-flowering phlomis I grow. In winter, crystallised by frost, it is equally striking. It's those large-lipped, toning cream and yellow flowers that give it such allure.

Close by in my garden lies the very similar but more invasive *Phlomis russeliana*. Where space allows, this coarser cream- and yellow-flowered phlomis could be allowed to roam, but it is an aggressive spreader – it invades my lawn with regularity – and self-seeds as well. Each dried head bears five whorls of flowers, and there is often an endearing tuft of two leaves at the very top of the plant when flowering. The stem grows up through the middle of the whorls. The lowest seedhead can measure 8cm (3in) across, but the others taper and narrow as the stem lengthens. *P. russeliana* must be planted with similar 'toughies' that it can't smother as it spreads. I mix it with the strong, substantial late summer flowering *Crocosmia masoniorum* and the robust *Acanthus spinosus*. All three plants reach about 1.2m (4ft) in height during summer, as they battle it out down a sunny path; in winter, their

LEFT *Frosted seedheads of* Crocosmia masoniorum, *taken in my own garden. This branched* Crocosmia *forms a strong silhouette.*

RIGHT *Prickly bracts protect the large seed capsules that follow acanthus blooms. Held high on long stems, they are especially handsome when touched by frost.*

contrasting leaf shapes provide strong structural interest. *C. masoniorum* has pleated, bright green leaves. The upright stems of bronze-orange, late-summer flowers mimic several birds in synchronised flight, while the bare seedheads in winter reveal the symmetrical splay of arching stems arranged in a curved herringbone pattern. It is a very pleasing plant, both in summer and winter.

Perhaps the most voguish of all phlomis is the mauve-pink tuberous *Phlomis tuberosa* 'Amazone', popularised by Piet Oudolf, but actually raised by the German plant breeder Ernst Pagels. This slender perennial produces whorls of flowers above pairs of long, nettle-green leaves in summer, and the wiry stems are very slim, straight and dark. In autumn the leaves die away, but the stiff stems remain. 'Amazone' blends with pennisetums and other late-season grasses and perennials, although it generally doesn't combine well with silvers. It is sterile and won't produce seed, and I think this sterility makes the flowers last longer.

HANDSOME ACANTHUS Acanthus seedheads go well with phlomis, matching them in their statuesque, stiff-stemmed gait. Their late-summer, hooded, purple and white flowers have a cool elegance and a useful longevity in the border. Shiny chestnut-brown seed capsules, which resemble pointed acorns in shine and shape, expand and are supported from below by a prickly bract that arches downwards. As winter wears on, these jagged bracts disintegrate to reveal an intricate tracery of veins held together by jagged edging.

In all my years of gardening I have never found a seed inside any of those pointed acorn-like acanthus capsules, despite thorough searches. But in the wilds of Greece, where the acanthus flowers early, it is possible to hear the capsules exploding as they discharge their seeds. British temperatures (at least where I live) seem to make this plant sterile.

Acathus spinosus is the most commonly grown acanthus and is the most reliable to flower. However, the nature of all acanthus is to flower spasmodically. In some years there may be five flower spikes, in others seven, and sometimes a mere three will head skywards. There is no rhyme or reason that I can fathom. Every summer I take a peek to see if any buds are emerging – these are visible from above, and resemble huge asparagus spears. Although flowering is erratic, the splendidly ornate leaves, darkly crinkled and cut, are handsome enough on their own, and this majestic plant should play a part in all but the smallest gardens. Although the leaves have gone by the winter, the striking seedheads remain.

If given sun and fertile soil, this plant does well and endures for years. Indeed, eradicating it is almost impossible, as the merest section of root grows back into a large plant within about four years or so. Other acanthus are either less majestic, as in the case of the shorter, pink- and white-flowered *Acanthus hungaricus*. Or they flower less well, for example *A. mollis*. All acanthus can be accommodated in shade, but at the expense of lots of flower.

SUMMER BLUES TO WINTER BROWNS

In addition to the Mediterranean aromatics, there are other sun-loving plants for well-drained situations that provide winter interest. They include the gentian-blue *Ceratostigma plumbaginoides*. The clusters of gentian-blue flowers appear in late summer and autumn, when the leaves are green, and are set on wiry stems that reach 1–1.2m (3–4ft) in height. The similar *C. willmottianum* is apparently even taller, although I haven't grown it. When autumn arrives, the foliage on *C. plumbaginoides* changes to warm red, and the rich brown seedheads – the shape and size of splayed sea thrift heads – stiffen on the ends of the stems. Sometimes a stray, late blue flower limps along with them, looking very poignant.

My *Ceratostigma plumbaginoides* resides on the sun-baked side of a tall red kniphofia called 'Prince Igor'. In late summer, the combination of taller-than-any-man, orange-red pokers, surrounded by a deep blue frill of ceratostigma flowers, never fails to satisfy me. It's further enhanced by several deep blue agapanthus, whose names I don't know. Blues are so few and far between that every gardener should have at least some of these evening stars shining out in the fading light.

The heights of my different agapanthus vary, but the foliage always dies back on mine, leaving a collection of straight green stems topped by a round arrangement of flattened green banana pods, suspended on radiating stems that jut outwards. They remind me of cars on a fairground ride, spun out by centrifugal force. Among the green pods, several paper-brown capsules split to reveal flat black seeds. This attractive combination of green, brown and black will endure until Christmas and beyond.

SWORDS AND SWIRLS Certain grass-leaved plants persist into winter, and look very effective growing among silver-leaved Mediterranean aromatics. These include those arching South African beauties, the dieramas, also known as angel's fishing rods. The easiest to grow is the tall *Dierama pulcherrimum*, a midsummer-flowering wand of swinging bells, usually in vivid pink. When these dieramas first appear, they send up a grass-like wiry stem that tops 2m (6ft), then an arch of pendant bells unfurls, followed by round and knobbly seedheads.

BELOW *Agapanthus seed-heads will withstand cold weather and they can persist in the open ground in well-drained soil.*

RIGHT *The swinging, grass-like heads of Dierama pulcherrimum are hung with decorative brown seeds.*

Dieramas shed their large brown seeds in early autumn, but the attractive seedheads remain atop slim, arching stems, catching the winter frost. The slender leaves also remain on the plant, providing structure and interest throughout the winter months. The leaves resemble those of irises, although they are tougher and narrower. In my garden, I have to remove all the stems in late summer, as they self-seed too copiously in my gravel, but on soil, dieramas are far less trouble. The best way to produce more dieramas is to sprinkle fresh seed over soil and then cover it with gravel; the seedlings will take around four or five years to flower.

A similar sheath of leaves is produced by some kniphofias, although they are softer than those of dieramas. I can recommend the lime-green *Kniphofia* 'Percy's Pride' as an attractive, thoroughly reliable variety. It begins flowering in early summer and keeps going until mid-autumn if it's really happy, reaching 1.2m (4ft). 'Bees' Lemon' is a good, slender lemon-yellow poker with a slightly shorter height of 1m (3ft); its buds are a cool, woodpecker-green. 'Wrexham Buttercup' is a fat, golden yellow poker that can top 1m (3ft), and 'Samuel's Sensation' is a lovely, tall red that is capable of reaching 1–1.2m (3–4ft). However, little can beat the late-summer exuberance of the 3–4m (10–13ft) high orange spikes of *K. uvaria* 'Nobilis'. The bonus of all these kniphofias is that in winter you have a fountain of leaf and you can leave the tall, gaunt stems, now devoid of flowers, to punctuate the air in defiance.

Generally, the thicker the leaf and the more substantial the poker, the easier they are to grow. There are several grassy, short, autumn-flowering pokers, for example forms of *Kniphofia galpinii*, but I have not found any of them long-lived and they can be reluctant to flower, perhaps needing more moisture than I can provide.

Wasps love poker nectar, and I'm rarely bothered with any of these creatures in the house, as they're all too busy sucking up the nectar (if you've ever knocked into one of the giant pokers on a summer's day, you'll be showered in the sugary stuff). The enemy of all pokers is the snail. In winter they lurk in the foliage, where they breed, and their offspring later chomp through the buds. Frisk the plants regularly and exterminate!

PINKS, PURPLES AND REDS Other sun-lovers you can rely on to provide winter interest are the fleshy-leaved sedums, which also need some moisture to perform well. The largest, flattest heads belong to the ice plant *Sedum spectabile*, a green-rosetted, substantial sedum with sugar-pink flowers. When winter comes, the pink flowerheads mature to wine-red and then to deep brown, and they will stay intact until next spring. 'Herbstfreude', previously known as 'Autumn Joy' and found in every garden in my childhood, is the most commonly grown sedum.

In recent years, the dark-leaved sedums have seduced me away from the green-leaved ones. *Sedum telephium* 'Matrona' is the most statuesque dark-leaved sedum. It looks as though it's on steroids – reaching well over 60cm (2ft) in height and has thick stems and huge, fleshy leaves (almost like those of *Opuntia* cacti) and rose-red flowers. It casts a real presence once planted, but looks unattractive and top-heavy in a garden-centre pot. Take it home, plant it in the garden, and this ugly duckling will flourish.

Sedum telephium subsp. *maximum* 'Atropurpurea' (doesn't that name make you love botanists!) produces foliage that turns from green to brown-purple, and the beautiful pink flowers fade to chocolate as winter approaches. It's more delicate and shorter than 'Matrona', reaching a height of 60cm (2ft). 'Vera Jameson' has similar coloration, but is a low-growing sprawler of alpine proportions.

Among the sedums, you could grow late summer flowering origanums, named forms of *Origanum laevigatum*. They have long, slender stems topped with a combination of tiny, pale pink flowers held in dark purple calices; these hold their colour, almost like sea lavender. There are several forms, but 'Herrenhausen' is one of the best. In winter, the sea-lavender-like seedheads take on a dark aubergine tint, bordering on black. These touches of dark purple or red add depth and sparkle among silver plants, which would look bland on their own.

The low-growing knapweed, *Serratula seoanei*, sends out low, fuzzy mauve flowers in late summer and early autumn. It prefers moisture and partial sun rather than the hottest, driest spot, and will add some winter interest when the flowers fade to leave upright heads that resemble ragged fat thistles on short stems.

The tight clusters of dark, pointed pods on slender stems produced by the Carthusian pink (*Dianthus carthusianorum*) are also highly pleasing. This species pink, easily raised from seed, bears clusters of cerise-pink, single flowers on stems 30cm (12in) high, between early summer and early autumn. They look like emaciated sweet Williams in structure, but the flowers emerge in succession from a tight, dark cluster of pointed, narrow buds. As the flowers fade they are replaced by slim, torpedo-shaped seedpods, arranged in the same compact way and similarly dark. They remain on the plant over winter.

ROBUST PERFORMERS There are plenty of robust, late-flowering plants that have good seedheads in winter; many of these look superb with tall, late-season grasses. *Hydrangea arborescens* 'Annabelle', for example, is an excellent winter performer. It grows on any soil, and is tough and drought-resistant. The individual flowers, which are made of four well-spaced papery bracts, combine to form a large, domed, Tiffany-lamp-shaped flowerhead. These are white when they appear, and then age to green-white in early autumn, before turning a warm brown as winter approaches. When low sun shines through, it highlights the tiny veins in the flowers. The flowerheads are held on stiff stems between 1.2 and 1.5m (4–5ft) high and, unlike some other *H. arborescens* cultivars, the heads of 'Annabelle' are not too heavy. There is no need to cut the stems down, just remove the flowers above the highest buds on each stem in early spring or mid-spring.

Hydrangea macrophylla cultivars are available in deep blues and pinks, but they are more demanding than *H. arborescens* 'Annabelle', needing a cool root run, moist, fertile soil and quite a lot of rainfall. They do best in milder, damper conditions.

Tall asters also mix well with taller grasses. The following varieties are all over 1m (3ft) high, flower in early autumn and, once they have finished flowering, their stiff stems are topped with fluffy clusters of white, downy seedheads that last into winter. *Aster laevis* 'Calliope' has dark foliage that intensifies the blue of the flowers, and reaches over 1.2m (4ft). There are also some good *A. novae-angliae* varieties, including the raspberry-pink 'Andenken an Alma Pötschke', the claret-red 'Primrose Upward', 'Harrington's Pink' and 'Purple Dome'. I am also a fan of the lovely blue *A.* 'Little Carlow', a shorter aster (about 80cm/2½ft high) that is studded with tiny blue flowers.

All these asters need some sun and moisture at the roots. An area of the garden that only attracts morning or afternoon sun is often perfect for asters, as the midday sun can dry them out. If you have the choice, opt for afternoon sun, because butterflies adore these jewel-box flowers and are more likely to

LEFT *The delicate, upward-reaching spokes of a fennel head are rimed in frost.*

ABOVE *The lacy remnants of Hydrangea arborescens 'Annabelle' persist all winter.*

be on the wing in the afternoon. Ideally, leave them to form large clumps. If you do divide asters or any other autumn-flowering perennial, the golden rule is to divide in spring, once they begin to grow away. Never divide them in autumn, when they've used all their energy in flower production.

One later aster, with a branched, low-growing stem, is the starry white *Aster lateriflorus* 'Horizontalis'. This is useful at the front of borders containing late perennials and other asters, as it only reaches 1m (3ft) at the most and is so late into flower that it almost breaches autumn and winter. In winter, it takes on the appearance of a miniature branched conifer blown to one side by the wind.

The vernonias are closely related to the asters. They have the same stiff stance and North American provenance. *Vernonia crinita* 'Mammuth' has wider, more vibrant purple heads than other vernonias that seem midway between a clustered aster and a fluffy eupatorium. Speaking of fluffy eupatoriums, they are often wishy-washy blue-pinks (surely the most unattractive colour in the garden), too invasive for most gardens, and they self-seed too. *Eupatorium purpureum* subsp. *maculatum* 'Atropurpureum', however, is highly recommended. It is far less invasive than other eupatoriums, and the dark maroon-pink flowers, which are borne from late summer to mid-autumn, are divine in autumn sunlight and make good, fluffy grey-white seedheads when winter descends.

Other perennials that look good later in the season are the tall yellow daisies, such as rudbeckias, which flower in late summer and early autumn. In winter, the stems are topped in black cones that resemble snuffed-out rockets; they take on a steely glimmer in frost and contrast well with fluffier heads.

The three rudbeckias of note for winter interest are the giant *Rudbeckia* 'Herbstsonne', a clump-forming, single yellow daisy with drooping ray petals, at 2.2m (7ft) tall, and the shorter, fully double yellow 'Goldquelle', a compact daisy that reaches only 1.2m (4ft). The third is a plant that inspires strong feelings, *R. maxima*. It has large, glaucous green leaves at the base and strong stems topped with garish, black-centred yellow daisies. It is extremely robust, almost coarse, demands moisture to survive, and appears to have a masculine strength – you either love it or loathe it.

Any of the annual Gloriosa daisies, selected forms of *Rudbeckia hirta*, will fade to leave strange black triangular cones. With their tall, stiff stems, 60–90cm (2–3ft) high, they certainly make an impact. Similarly, the excellent low-growing perennial *R. fulgida* var. *deamii*, sometimes called black-eyed Susan, has smaller, dark-centred yellow flowers that fade in the same way. Heleniums and echinaceas, though shorter in stature, will also give you a stem topped with a cone. The short, floriferous *Echinacea* 'Kim's Knee High' is a particularly useful plant for the front of a border.

Two other late-season performers make perfect partners in moisture-retentive soil: *Helianthus* 'Lemon Queen' and the thick-stemmed *Aconitum carmichaelii* 'Arendsii'. Both of these plants grow to about 2m (6ft) if they are given good soil, and both are self-supporting perennials that don't need staking and continue to look good into winter. In late summer, *Helianthus* 'Lemon Queen' bears small daisy flowers, which are held vertically on a tight, clump-forming rootstock. As the sun moves round, the flowers turn to face it, so the afternoon sun should face this plant, otherwise you'll be looking at the backs of the daisies' heads. The Arendsii aconitum has large, hooded, pastel mauve-blue flowers in early autumn, set against large leaves. The stems are grey-green and downy, and the violet-blue of the aconitum sets off 'Lemon Queen' perfectly. As winter descends, the combination is just as winning – the spent, snapdragon spikes of the aconitums reaching over 2m (6ft) high and the black-starred helianthus daisies, which can be even taller, forming a clump of close stems topped by dark disks. If you want to add a bit more lemon to the border – this time at a lower level – the refined golden rod hybrid x *Solidaster luteus* 'Lemore', up to 1m (3ft) high, has substantial lemon heads that pick up the yellow of 'Lemon Queen' from midsummer to early autumn; from mid-autumn into winter they will also give you a gritty, dark seedhead.

LEFT *Echinaceas, or cone flowers, shed their petals and leave the thimble-like cone supported by a round collar.*

You could create several bold verticals in the winter garden by growing some veronicastrums, provided your water table is high enough. I have succeeded with the aptly named *Veronicastrum* 'Pointed Finger' – the tapered flower, and then seedhead, waggle towards you Lord Kitchener style.
The rose-pink 'Apollo' and the mauve-blue 'Fascination' both point straight to heaven. All reach 1.2m (4ft). I urge everyone to plant more veronicastrums. They look especially striking between phloxes at the front of grassy borders, and we don't use them nearly enough.

Other verticals that could be drifted through a late-season border of grasses and perennials to provide structure and line in the winter garden include the tall, airy *Verbena bonariensis,* beloved by comma butterflies. In my garden it doesn't self-seed and overwinter well – every year I raise new plants and pot them out in midsummer, for the early autumn spectacular – but in other places, particularly in gravel, they self-seed easily. By winter the stems may be leaning at an angle, but the flat flowers will remain intact, providing little platforms for frost and snow.

RIGHT *The branching head of* Verbena bonariensis *is an everlasting element in a late-season border.*

Bold, spiky plants have a dramatic effect, leading the eye skywards to make a strong statement. They unite surrounding planting schemes and are particularly useful when combined with finely textured foliage, which lacks definition without a strongly shaped plant sculpture. This effect works in winter or summer and many tall, late-season grasses can be used in the same dynamic way.

plumes and spikes

Late-season grasses contribute greatly to the winter garden, and are ideal for planting through late-flowering perennials. Most require a well-drained soil, but miscanthus and molinias cope well with heavier soils. Their flowerheads are stunning in autumn, and then they continue to dazzle as winter arrives. As the surrounding perennials retreat, they make even more of an impact on the eye. They are one group of plants I just couldn't manage without.

The soft ponytail grass, *Stipa tenuissima* – a moving, fibre-optic grass that fades to sun-bleached canvas threads – will make your border shine on short, winter days, and the taller *S. capillata* stretches its long, filaments heaven-ward to form fine, regularly branched verticals. Although past its prime in winter, the giant feather grass, *S. gigantea*, continues to arch out from the clump, making its presence felt in the winter garden. The straw-yellow spikelets, on tall stems about 1.5m (5ft) high, create a lovely light, gauzy, shimmering veil to peer through. Plants like this, used as common themes woven through a border, can unite a whole swathe of the garden in every season.

Miscanthus: king of grasses

The finest grassy winter heads belong to the late-season grasses. Of these, the undisputed champion is the plumed *Miscanthus sinensis*, commonly called Chinese silver grass or eulalia grass. There are so many named forms of *M. sinensis* to choose from – a recent trial held at the RHS Wisley garden, between 1998 and 2001, gathered together over a hundred varieties. These miscanthus varied in

BELOW Pennisetum villosum (switch grass) produces striking white-bristled heads in late autumn that will persist into winter. Its attractiveness compensates for the fact that it will need to be reseeded each year.

height, and in the colour and shape of their leaves and plumes. Some were over 4m (13ft) high, others were one-third of the size. Some leaves had horizontal banding, others linear variegation. Plume colour ranged from wine-red to palest silver-white, and the shape of the plumes varied from closed, upward-facing cockades to Afghan-hound-like-ears flapping in the wind.

I have a real passion for miscanthus, and can't imagine a garden without them – alleluya for the eulalia I chant! I have at least 11 in the autumn border. They're rubbing shoulders with tall, late herbaceous perennials and that most accommodating upright shrub, *Cotinus coggygria* 'Royal Purple'. The rounded, claret-red leaves emerge late and stay in position until late autumn, becoming occasionally flecked in lipstick pink. The cotinus foliage adds luminosity to the fading plumes of my miscanthus – although some are red-plumed at first, within six weeks or so they fade to a rust-brown, and the silvers lighten to almost white. I think the mellow, ruby-port tones of fading coggygria lift the decadently faded palette of late-season grasses better than anything else. I have planted the true-blue midsummer-flowering *Clematis* 'Perle d'Azur' to wend through the claret leaves. Pruning cotinus in late spring will make the leaves larger and encourage the production of strong, attractive stems for winter.

The heads of *Miscanthus sinensis* have the same fluffy texture as pampas grass (*Cortaderia selloana*) but lack the upright stiffness and solidity, allowing them to tremble and flutter in the low winter sun. Miscanthus also produce a tight clump of vertical leaf in summer and this makes them a perfect foil for tall purple alliums (such as 'Purple Sensation'), late spring tulips in clear colours and even dark astrantias. However, the leaves of miscanthus die away by winter.

Miscanthus seedheads can be left on until mid- to late winter, but then it's best to cut them away at the base because, if left any longer, the new growth comes up through the old stems. When deciding which miscanthus to grow, consider where you live, because flowering times vary. For instance, in warm areas of England, such as the south-west, many *Miscanthus sinensis* varieties produce flower spikes in late summer. However, in my garden in middle England, I have to wait until early autumn. For anyone in a cold area, there are a number of early-flowering varieties.

It was the late-season flowering in northern temperate areas that held back miscanthus breeding for years, because plants grown outside rarely, if ever, set seed. It was only when the German plant breeder, Ernst Pagels, used a heated greenhouse to extend the growing season of *Miscanthus sinensis* 'Gracillimus' that it produced a hybrid seed crop. That variable batch of seedlings, raised in the late 1950s from the first cross, laid the foundation for many new miscanthus varieties.

Some of the tall miscanthus make large substantial clumps, so choose carefully if space is limited. Among my favourite tall and substantial white-silver tops are *Miscanthus sinensis* 'Roland', a giant at about 2.8m (9ft), which

ABOVE *Miscanthus provide a delicate froth of attractive plumes that will last long after the leaves have died away.*

holds airy, elegant plumes high up above the foliage. On close inspection, each plume looks as though it has been crimped by hair irons. 'Silberfeder' is not as tall, reaching just over 2m (6ft), and the denser plumes are held more vertically, pointing upwards, just slightly above the foliage. Scorn is often poured on 'Silberfeder', and detractors say it breaks up early. However, this is my earliest miscanthus to flower, and for that reason I would recommend it highly.

The early-to-flower *Miscanthus sinensis* 'Ferner Osten' (sometimes labelled 'Far East'), one of Pagel's varieties, has dull red plumes that age to silver; it reaches about 1.5m (5ft) tall. 'China' is the same height, and the narrow red flowers are held on long stems. 'Kleine Fontäne' produces masses of slender, silky red plumes, tightly held together by the foliage, and it also reaches 1.5m (5ft). 'Malepartus', at 2m (6ft) high, is also highly regarded, with purple-red flowerheads that arch slightly downwards. Other notable varieties include 'Flamingo', a rose-red-plumed miscanthus, reaching 2m (6ft) in height, with an erect habit, graceful foliage and rose-coloured, silvery soft drooping flowers. 'Kaskade' has cascading rose-coloured flowers held well above the leaves, and if a tall red is desired, 'Grosse Fontäne' produces tall red flowerheads, also held above the foliage and reaching 2.5–3m (8–10ft). All of these darker-plumed miscanthus fade to a deeper, duller brown-grey colour as the season goes on, but their striking shapes remain a prominent feature of the winter border.

VARIEGATED MISCANTHUS There are also variegated miscanthus, grown primarily for their impressive foliage. Although the foliage of most dies down in winter, the softly plumed, open seedheads are a feature in the winter border, and bring a sense of movement to the garden as they flutter in the wind.

If I had to recommend one variegated miscanthus for the smaller garden it would be the fine-leaved green and white *Miscanthus sinensis* 'Morning Light', which is evergreen so provides a presence all year round. It produces a light, upright fountain of needle-thin leaves, glimmering as a pale green stook in full sun, and has tiny, feathery open heads of soft beige flowers in mid-autumn, fading to white by winter. The diminutive 'Yakushima Dwarf' is also lovely, making a 1.2m (4ft) high mound of fine foliage, punctuated by lots of upward-facing tight tassels held almost among the leaves. I have seen this grown in grass (as neatly spaced individuals) at Goodnestone Park in Kent, looking superbly regular.

RIGHT *The white-silver fronds of* Miscanthus sinensis *seedheads glimmer in gentle winter light.*

Some of the taller miscanthus are horizontally banded in erratic yellow markings: *Miscanthus sinensis* 'Zebrinus' produces a cascading fountain of barred leaf. This old variety, grown by Gertrude Jekyll at her Munstead Wood garden in Surrey, has proved worthy in the garden for almost a hundred years. A newer form with similar markings, 'Strictus', is very upright and stiff in shape. It's neater, but to me it lacks a certain flow.

The new *Miscanthus sinensis* var. *condensatus* 'Cosmopolitan' reaches 1.5m (5ft) and has deep green leaves edged in cream. I have found it slow to make a clump here, and it hasn't attempted to flower, but it will in milder areas – at RHS Garden in Wisley, for example, it has produced silver flower plumes. 'Cabaret', which I haven't grown but do admire, has wide leaves with linear variegation running down the midribs.

Vertical companions

Grasses to weave among your miscanthus include the ramrod-straight *Calamagrostis* x *acutiflora* 'Karl Foerster', which sends up a bundle of tight stems to a height of 2m (6ft). The open, feathery flowerheads appear in mid-summer, but by autumn they have reduced to form rust-brown sky rockets that persist until late winter. It is the only grass to give this straight up-and-down set of closely allied stems topped in russet brown. You have to space several specimens of this plant through your autumn or grass border; one clump forms such a strong silhouette, it looks odd on its own. The variegated green and cream form, 'Overdam', is gentler and shorter, and looks most effective planted in close groups of five and seven.

A much shorter, fluffier species, *Calamagrostis brachytricha* reaches about 60–100cm (2–3ft) high and produces pyramidal violet-pink flowerheads in early autumn. By winter, these have faded to pale straw. The fine stems and delicate triangular heads persist, despite their delicate appearance. This grass, which is happiest in moist shade, is one of the best late-season, low-growing grasses to use along shady paths.

Open, airy heads

Tall, beaded grasses with open, airy heads set up a fine contrast when interspersed among more substantial plumes. The tall forms of *Molinia caerulea* are grouped together under subsp. *arundinacea*, but the heads can vary from substantial heavy heads, such as those of 'Skyrocket', to finely beaded ones. 'Transparent' reigns supreme for me. This tall grass reaches up to 1.5m (5ft) and has open heads and stems that appear jet black in sunlight. It creates a gauzy haze of shining seeds, which you only see when the sun strikes them, and will remain intact into late winter.

The shorter panicums, which reach 1–1.2m (3–4ft), have open, airy seed-heads that endure into winter. The foliage of these grasses can be somewhat raggedy in winter, but if you grow them among late-seasonal perennials and other grasses you can hide the leaves. *Panicum virgatum* 'Heavy Metal', with blue-grey foliage, is the best variety; there are also red-brown forms. Panicums demand warm conditions and moist soil, and tend to lose their beaded look as the shortest day approaches.

Fluffy plumes

Although I couldn't recommend pampas grass (*Cortaderia selloana*) for a mixed border, because it flowers so late and is so top-heavy and stiffly imposing, there is an airier, early form. *Cortaderia richardii*, a New Zealand native, flowers in midsummer, but demands moisture to perform well and it may not survive in colder areas of the country.

Although I think of all the grasses I've mentioned previously as being truly perennial (with the possible exception of *Cortaderia richardii*), the bottlebrush pennisetums are best thought of as tender annuals in gardening terms. In autumn, they send out fluffy heads that persist only until early winter. Despite this, I use them a lot. The annual *Pennisetum villosum* is grown every year from seed. Prick out clumps of seedlings into 8cm (3in) pots and plant them outside in midsummer. I tend to use this white, fluffy grass with a low-growing branched purple verbena, *Verbena rigida*. This is similar to the taller, leggier *V. bonariensis*, but is only 30cm (12in) high, and is a more intense, richer blue-purple shade. It is easy to grow from seed, and is perennial in good winters.

You can also sow the tender fountain grass, *Pennisetum setacum*, in spring. This produces stunning fluffy heads, but it is tender and cannot be planted out until the frosts have passed and won't come through a harsh winter. Even if it doesn't reshoot the following spring, it is still worth considering as it provides a winter presence.

Several pennisetums are listed as perennials and these include the hardiest of all, the fountain grass, *Pennisetum alopecuroides*. 'Hameln', a fuzzy fawn and green caterpillar-like grass with fine dark hairs, is the most widely available variety and it has come through several winters. But I have seen some exciting red, getting on for black forms too. 'Mouldry' and 'National Arboretum' are both listed as black; they will only flower in warm summers. Some pennisetums will flower in late summer. *P. macrourum*, for example, produces slender, pencil-thick, fluffy beige tails that measure 15cm (6in) in length. These often fade in colour as cold weather takes charge, but the long stems still persist. All perennial pennisetums have been short-lived for me, lasting on average four years.

LEFT *The finely beaded heads of* Molinia caerulea *subsp.* arundinacea *'Transparent' glimmer like tiny jet beads.*

leafy
fillers

3

Much of the garden tends to resemble a black and white chalk and charcoal sketch in winter, but this means that any solid blocks of leaf stand out much more strongly in winter than summer.

splashes of colour

Shaped and topiarised evergreens – for example a pair of box balls positioned on either side of a path or at the top of steps – make stunning winter features. They bring structure, definition and interest to the garden, and will make a far greater impact on the eye than in summer, when you barely notice them as there are so many other distractions around. Warm, true-green evergreens with high-gloss leaves are at their most glowing and radiant in good light conditions. In shadier areas, you may wish to use variegated evergreens to lift a scheme and provide contrast, as deep green leaves in dense shade tend to look drab and uninteresting. Similarly, golden leaves are ideal for brightening up darker, gloomy areas of the garden; indeed, most golden foliage plants require a shady site as the leaves scorch in bright sunshine. Dark-coloured foliage, for instance in deep plum or purple, is also useful in the garden in good light conditions; it focuses the eye and creates a striking contrast with any pale colour nearby.

True evergreens are not the only consideration, because many early-flowering woodland plants arm themselves with leaves in the preamble to flowering, and this ground-hugging foliage stands out well against the soil. Many of these plants grow under shrubs and trees and are hidden away in summer by summer-flowering perennials. However, their leafy winter presence is welcome, being both good to look at and providing shelter for insects and small animal life.

LEFT *Variegated evergreens, such as Ilex altaclarensis 'Golden King' are sure to lift any dark corner in the garden.*

RIGHT *These swirling jellyfish, provided by Carex comans bronze form, break up the small heathers and link the eye to the bare brown twigs.*

PREVIOUS PAGES *Marylyn Abbott's Walled Garden at West Dean in Hampshire uses a formal arrangement of clipped box. The ironwork at the heart of the garden demands a mixture of shapes from mound and whirligig to pointed rectangle.*

It is no accident that our ancestors looked at rich green leaves (our native yew, holly, box and mistletoe) and awarded them a magical status. After all, they kept the flame of life going over winter and sheltered the mythical Green Man, a symbol of ever-lasting life. On the shortest day, these plants were gathered in and placed near the hearth in rites that have pre-Christian roots.

rich bolts of green

Green makes a far greater impact on the garden in winter than in summer – it stands out more when the sun is lower in the sky, and takes on a warmer hue. In the garden, we can exploit this winter richness of green in several ways – we can plant an evergreen hedge, clip slow-growing box, holly or yew into tight shapes, plant a steep bank with evergreen ground cover, or add larger evergreens to a boundary wall. Structural evergreens will keep the garden going over winter, and will help make the garden work visually: they can emphasise symmetry and design when placed in a pattern, or they can make solid shapes that carry the eye across the garden. Nature will thank us for it too, as evergreens provide much-needed winter shelter for insects, birds and small animal life.

Our gardens will also look better for these rich bolts of green. I can remember Margery Fish (1888–1969) – a famous cottage gardener who popularised hardy geraniums, snowdrops and pulmonarias at East Lambrook Manor in Somerset – writing about an argument she had with her husband Walter. He insisted that she plant structural evergreens among her cottage garden borders, but she argued against it. Domestic harmony at threat, Margery reluctantly concurred (as only females will) and allowed Walter to plant several in strategic places. Years later she was forced to concede that Walter had been perfectly correct. His evergreens kept the garden going in winter and made the garden work visually.

BELOW *These golden columns of leaf, from Taxus baccata 'Fastigiata Aureomarginata', take the eye skywards. Any slender vertical should be a repeat theme.*

Handsome specimens

There are several large evergreen shrubs that could be grown as handsome single specimens or used against a boundary to provide interest in winter. In summer, you can add your own touches of red among them by planting the herbaceous *Potentilla* 'Gibson's Scarlet', a green-leaved member of the strawberry family that produces wands of simple red, five-petalled flowers, and *Viburnum opulus* 'Compactum', which produces red berries in late summer that often stay on the plant until early winter or beyond.

Viburnum tinus, also known as laurestinus, was an old Victorian favourite. There are two named forms of note: 'Gwenllian', which has deep pink flowers buds and white flowers, and 'Eve Price', which is more compact, with carmine buds opening to pink-tinged flowers. Both flower from early winter onwards, and can be trimmed back in late spring, after flowering, if needed. *V. tinus* is unscented, but the clusters of flowers are weather-resistant and very welcome. The big advantage of this large rounded shrub, 3 x 3m (10 x 10ft), is its ability to grow against fences and in shade.

Osmanthus will also grow in the dankest, darkest corners. There are two forms – *Osmanthus* x *burkwoodii* and *O. delavayi*. Both resemble unclipped privet hedges and have white, tubular, fragrant flowers in early spring; *O. delavayi* is the finer of the two. Their foliage is deep green, and they will add depth to a shady area or hide a fence or other eyesore. Mine grows in a corner where two fence posts meet.

My all-time favourite evergreen to brighten up those all-too-short winter days is *Aucuba japonica*. The large oval leaves are laurel-like, but it's their ability to make roundly dense mounds of interesting leaves, even in deep shade, that win me over. These positively glow in winter, although the soft tops can be damaged in very hard weather. They also grow quickly, and an aucuba will make a feature in five years (or less), while most hollies take ten. There are several varieties, and a male and female mix should produce berries. The variegated forms still glow green and include the widely available, spotted female 'Crotonifolia', and 'Golden King', a male with smaller, more brashly variegated leaves. There are also pure green-leaved forms, including the slender-leaved female f. *longifolia* and dark green female 'Hillieri'. The variegated forms are more often grown and, as they tend to be lightly spotted in gold, they do light up boundaries, while also giving that necessary bolt of winter green.

RIGHT Viburnum tinus thrives in shade and provides pretty pink-white flowers. 'Gwenllian', pictured here, has the pinkest flowers.

Covering walls

A warm wall is the perfect place to shelter slightly tender wall shrubs, and when we think of warm walls we tend to imagine south-facing aspects. Yet I have found north-facing walls can support slightly tender leafy plants too. They are sheltered from our prevailing south-westerly winds in most parts of the British Isles, so most rainfall doesn't reach a north wall. They get little sun, which prevents any damaging freeze-and-quick-thaw problems. And north walls provide a constant temperature because house or brick walls hold warmth.

Such a north-facing wall would be perfect for *Garrya elliptica*, a large North American evergreen that unfurls long, light grey-green tasselled catkins in midwinter. Prune it early in the year to avoid cutting out next year's catkins. Another plant that could be used for a north-facing wall (although a west-facing wall might be better) is that rampant evergreen magnolia with the large, high-gloss leaves, *Magnolia grandiflora*. Some forms have a chestnut-brown, powdery underside to the green leaves. 'Samuel Sommer' is my preferred selection, and this is also meant to be hardier than many others too. The cream-white flowers open to form cup-shaped blooms and can appear from early summer until late autumn. One of the things I like about this shrub is the way it rations out its flowers throughout the warmer parts of the year and doesn't just give us just one glorious throw of the dice.

Drimys winteri is another high-gloss evergreen that could be tucked away against a sheltered wall. In winter the leaves are neat, shiny and green, and the ivory star-shaped flowers appear all at once, a profusion of white in late spring or early summer. This shrub is more likely to spread outwards than upwards.

Clipped and shaped evergreens

Clipped evergreens can be used in several ways, and they are very much a matter of personal taste. You can use simply clipped evergreens to add style and elegance to the garden, announcing your intention of being in control and pushing against the more *laissez faire* style of the cottage garden. Clipped hedges and topiary can also add intimacy, something that the Arts and Crafts designers understood well. At Rodmarton Manor, in Gloucestershire, a garden that is open to the public, you can see good examples of how clipped evergreens are used to create feelings of enclosure and extend the house into the garden. On a less serious level, topiary can inject a real sense of fun. One gardener I know has created a menagerie of animals along a path – there's a bear, a mouse, a cat and a camel. In recent years, even some stately homes have incorporated this sense of fun into the clipped hedges and trees, and ancient yew hedges have had round windows cut into their length, creating cheeky glimpses of the landscape beyond.

ABOVE *The aptly named coat tassel bush, Garrya elliptica 'James Roof' will thrive in a shady spot. Its greyish green catkins turn silvery as they age.*

All the best shrubs for topiary are slow-growing, and this means that they need only one annual trim, and will then keep their shape for the rest of the year.

BOX AND YEW TOPIARY The form of box we most often topiarise is *Buxus sempervirens* 'Suffruticosa'. It has small-leaved, dense growth, ideal for clipping. Traditionally, this clipping was undertaken in early summer on Derby Day, when well-to-do families were away at Ascot for the week. There was a good practical reason for this too: young box foliage is scorched by frost and should only be clipped when danger of late frost has passed; for the same reason, you should not clip box after late summer. If new growth does turn brown, rub the unsightly foliage away with your fingers – box is tough and will recover.

Simple box cones, spirals, cubes or domes can be shaped by brave amateurs, and you can use string and canes as guides. I have a very poor eye for pruning and cutting, but box nurseries tell me that they often have staff who are naturals – they issue them with one-handed sheep clippers willingly – yet others are less handy and they have to hide the clippers from them. Like everything in life there's only one way to find out the bitter truth, get stuck in and have a go.

If you're starting from scratch (and on a budget), buy a healthy-looking box plant from a traditional supplier, hopefully someone who takes cuttings and grows their own. The fungal box disease, *Cylindrocladium*, seems to be much more prevalent in imported, tunnel-raised box, grown under glass in warm, not-very-ventilated conditions. Infected plants develop bare, twiggy

BELOW *Rodmarton Manor, in Gloucestershire, is a garden in the Arts and Crafts style. This avenue of clipped yew is at its best in winter.*

ends and then die. Once you have selected a healthy specimen, take cuttings so that you can increase your stock.

When I first started gardening, I tried to economise on the price of three box plants, which at that time seemed beyond my purse. Instead, I bought three bushy honeysuckles, *Lonicera nitida* 'Baggesen's Gold', and shaped them into perfect balls to add winter presence to my gravel garden. My 'Baggesen's Gold' grew all year round (even in winter) and I needed to trim them every month to keep the effect of perfectly shaped roundels going. Instead of growing evenly all round, they sent out long, stray stems 12cm (30in) or so in length, which meant regular trimming to keep them looking good. They proved a false economy, costing me a great deal in terms of time and energy, and I wished I'd had the initial sense to stretch to box in the first place, regardless of the price.

Like box, yew can also be cut into almost any shape. One that is grown for its naturally erect, columnar habit is the slender yew (*Taxus baccata* 'Fastigiata'), also known as the Irish yew – a female tree often found in churchyards. Gardeners are often tempted to plant a matching pair, but so far my strategically placed pairs have never matched. One is always taller and fatter than the other

growing box

IT'S A GREAT TEMPTATION WHEN YOU MOVE TO A GARDEN TO PLANT lots of box, enclosing your borders, adding box balls, spirals and mopheads. However, box is slow-growing, and buying largish box trees is an expensive exercise. Raising your own box plants is one option that keeps costs down, but do think carefully before you embark on planting too many in the present climate – box blight is now very prevalent, and the effects are heartbreaking, because the only course of treatment is to destroy and burn your treasured plants and replant something else.

Growing box in containers

Simple terracotta pots or wooden tubs of box can be widely used in the garden and have the added advantage of being moveable feasts. However, box foliage, when short of water and nutrients, takes on a metallic olive-tree glimmer look and loses its deep-green lustre. To avoid this, containerised box needs regular feeding and watering during the growing season. This needn't be onerous. Use slow-release fertiliser, which can be bought in cone-form. These can be pushed down into the soil around the plant twice a year.

Planting close to box

Box is a shallow-rooted plant that drains the moisture out of the soil. This makes it difficult to plant up box-lined beds in drier areas of the country or in sunny parterres. Many head gardeners resort to using bedding schemes. In spring, wallflowers, forget-me-nots and tulips work well. In summer, the blue *Salvia* 'Indigo

Spires' or bedding penstemons will thrive. Annuals also work well in box beds.

Taking box cuttings

You can increase your stock of box plants quite easily by taking cuttings. Look for semi-ripe wood, which is new growth that has begun to harden off. Tear these shoots off the parent plant, and you will have a small heel at the base of the cutting. Trim off the wispy bit at the base of the cutting with a clean, sharp knife and remove any nearby leaves. Then cut out the top tip of the cutting.

You can place these cuttings in pots of gritty compost and leave them somewhere shady, for instance in a cold frame, until next spring. Alternatively, you could use a heated propagator to speed up the process. You can also line a slim trench in the garden with horticultural sand and place your cuttings in this trench. Leave them undisturbed for one year before potting them up.

– and yes, I do have a Little and Large couple and can't decide how to fatten one up, or whether to reduce the other. There are also fine golden forms of yew, including 'Elegantissima', which are used to add texture and relief among dark greens. If yews are trimmed in late summer, they will still look neat into winter.

At Levens Hall, in Cumbria, both yew and box topiary are grown on a grand scale. The layout of the green trees was designed by Guillaume Beaumont in 1694, and there are 19th-century additions of golden yew. The topiary, in the form of chess pieces, a judge's wig, an umbrella, peacocks and Queen Elizabeth and her maids, take six weeks of trimming. Gardeners with good soil should be able to train the scarlet climber, *Tropaeolum speciosum*, up their yew trees (as they do at Levens Hall, Hidcote and many other great gardens) – a reminder that red and green are the most potent colour combination of all.

CLIPPED HOLLIES   There are some superb green-leaved hollies to choose from, many of which will shine and glow at the winter solstice, whether berried or not. Varieties of our eagle-taloned native, *Ilex aquifolium*, are often perfect for topiarising, but many also make fine pyramids or roundels when left to their own devices. Remember that varieties vary in habit and growth rate, and that the best advice on suitability comes from

holly specialists, who offer a wide range and know their plants. Also, bear in mind that hollies are best planted young.

The looser, more rangy hybrid, *Ilex* x *altaclerensis*, is perfect as a mophead. When the plant is young, remove all the lower branches and shape the remaining top branches into a lollipop head. Although this takes time, it's extremely effective. Nurseries specialising in mature specimens usually stock mophead hollies. 'Golden King' (a female berrier) is one of the best of the *altaclerensis* forms for making a mophead. 'Belgica Aurea' has a different growth habit, forming a conical tree when left to its own devices.

Elegant Georgian terraces or smart town houses suit formal or symmetrical arrangements of hollies, and containerised topiary in simple straight pots can be used to great effect. Clipped hollies can, however, also be used in a more informal manner. At Eastgrove Cottage in Worcestershire, I have seen large, often variegated, hollies shaped into cones and pyramids and grown in grass in wild parts of the garden. This arrangement suits the rural setting and introduces some elements of focus and structure.

LEFT *Clipped roundels of variegated holly, and green and golden yew set within a box edging, look so much more stylish than a hedge.*

There are some spectacular clipped hollies at Brodsworth Hall near Doncaster in Yorkshire – an English Heritage Grade 1 Victorian garden full of clipped evergreens of every type. Here, they use a whole range – holly, laurel, bay, box and yew – and arrange them in borders dedicated to greenery; each is precision in late summer. The variegated varieties add shade and light among the rich green textures. Make sure you intersperse variegated leaves with plain green, as too many variegated plants grown close together looks too busy, almost like a rash.

Clipped hollies tend to have their berries cut off, as they need clipping in midwinter, when the holly is virtually at a standstill, or in late summer. This is because new holly growth can be damaged by frost.

Evergreen hedging

You may like to have a run of evergreen hedging to give structure to the garden and provide a screen or boundary. However, make sure you never truncate a good view if there's a landscape beyond. One of the handsomest hedging plants in winter is the laurel (*Prunus laurocerasus*), also known as cherry laurel. It's one of the brashest greens and can grow underneath overhanging trees without suffering one jot. It seems equally at home in the country, or in the town, but will not thrive on shallow chalk. This tall hedge, which can reach 6m (20ft) in height, is probably too spacious for small gardens. It can be cut in late spring or in late summer.

A yew hedge (*Taxus baccata*) will enhance any garden. Yew is generally thought of as a plant for stately homes – whether this misconception is to do with style or just the notion that yew takes a hundred years to mature, I do not know, but the fact is that they will make a feature in about ten years. There are many gardeners who rarely move, having created their own personal Eden, so ten years is not excessive for a hedge that needs trimming only once a year, in late summer, and will live for hundreds of years or more. My great gardening regret is that I have planted so little yew in my own gardens.

Yew has the edge over any other conifer hedging because it has the ability to regenerate from bare wood. Your *Lleylandii* hedge may be quick-growing and, if well maintained, may look good for 20 or 30 years; but you will never be able to cut it back to bare wood, only trim it back to leaf. Also, yew will thrive on both chalk and on acid soils, which is pretty unusual in the plant world. However, be aware that it is toxic to grazing animals, and this may be important if fields are on your boundary.

The secret behind creating a quick yew hedge is to prepare the soil well, plant small, bare-root specimens in late winter, about 1m (3ft) high, and then water them with a nitrogen-rich, soluble plant food throughout the growing season (from mid-spring to late summer) every fortnight. Don't waterlog them though, as yews prefer well-drained soil. Leave any trimming for at least eight years, and then just reduce the top of the hedge to allow the sides to grow together, filling in the gaps. Ideally, trim your yew hedge in late summer, and it will look immaculate in winter.

CLOUD HEDGES Some hedges or edging can billow and curve, rather than form straight lines. *Buxus sempervirens* 'Suffruticosa' is widely grown for parterres and shaping, but it doesn't always have to be straight-edged. Cloud-

BELOW *Bumpy hedges with wavy lines look sensational with a delicate covering of frost.*

pruned box trees adorn the Royal Palace in Bangkok, but could look at home in your garden too. Yew is also ideal for wavy-edged hedges – the misshapen hedges at the National Trust's Montacute House, in Somerset, and at Bramdean House in Hampshire, for example, are whale-like structures rather than straight-edged chic. At Bramdean, the Second World War meant a dearth of gardeners agile enough to trim the top of the hedges (which involved balancing on a high plank) and seven years of war-time neglect created a monstrous being at the front, which is so much more interesting than a straight hedge. Holly hedges can also be cloud cut.

ABOVE *Of all the skimmias, 'Kew Green' is the most versatile, with its handsome, high-gloss, green foliage and conical heads of scented cream flowers.*

Low-level greens

You may not have room for huge yews or have centuries to shape them, but several smaller shrubs can add those glimmers of warm green instead. The smallest of all is a dome-shaped hebe with tiny leaves, which makes a rounded mound of 30cm (12in) or more. It is often called *Hebe* 'Green Globe' or 'Emerald Green' but is correctly named 'Emerald Gem'. This New Zealander was found in the Ruahine Mountains in 1970 and is superb, whether in the ground or in a container, as it provides good rich colour, soft foliage and texture. It prefers an open, airy position, as do so many New Zealanders.

I am also fond of *Skimmia* x *confusa* 'Kew Green', which will give you evergreen foliage and conical heads of buds throughout winter that eventually open to creamy white, fragrant flowers by mid-spring. This small, mound-forming, very slow-growing skimmia, reaching 1m (3ft) high at most, has glossy green foliage and will do well in shade, either in a container or in the ground. These shady conditions also suit our native laurel spurge (*Daphne laureola*), a low-growing, compact, branching shrub, up to 60cm (2ft) high, with rich rosettes of leaf that produce heads of sweetly fragrant green flowers from late winter to early spring. This is very good with plum hellebores, which can be sombre on their own. The larger, shade-loving *Skimmia laureola* forms a mound 1m (3ft) high and wide, and has high-gloss light green leaves. The conical cream-green flowers appear in mid- to late spring and are highly popular with bees. This very long-lived evergreen can be cut back as the flowers fade, to keep a tight, round shape.

Pachysandra terminalis is a high-gloss, low-level green filler for awkward spots, although only on lime-free soil. My garden has seen several off to an early grave, so instead I grow the sword-like fountains of the stinking gladwyn (*Iris foetidissima*) and the divided foliage of another attractively named native, the stinking hellebore (*Helleborus foetidus*). Both tolerate deep shade and can be hidden away in the depths of the garden during summer. In winter, they

re-emerge and the iris produces a thick fountain of leaf and berried pods, which open to reveal large red fruits. I also have an orange-berried form. The hellebore has clusters of small, lime-green bells, prettily edged in maroon, plus a strong stem of divided dark foliage. The stinking gladwyn produces seedlings, which must be weeded out if in the wrong place.

There is also a low-growing euphorbia with good green winter foliage – *Euphorbia amygdaloides* var. *robbiae*, often sold as Mrs Robb, after the Victorian lady who spotted it growing in Turkey and smuggled it back in a hat box. This plant has rosettes of dark leaves on stiff 30cm (12in) high stems. These unfurl to pro-duce acid-yellow flowerheads in mid-spring and make a good double act with bluebells in a wild area of the garden. In winter, the foliage is very welcome and you get spring zing when the flowers appear. Remove the spent stems after flowering, to encourage next year's new growth. All spring-flowering euphorbias need this treatment, because next year's flowers will be borne on the new basal shoots. The sticky sap of all euphorbias is highly irritating to the skin and damaging to the eyes and, before cutting any euphorbias back, always arm yourself with goggles, long sleeves and trousers. I know it sounds extreme, but I spent a night in hospital in extreme discomfort after I deftly removed a stem with my secateurs while waiting for a friend to arrive for supper.

Pure green can be provided on the ground by planting periwinkles, or vincas, but only if you've room for a spreader with no conscience. Vincas send out overground runners (rather like strawberry plants), so they do require space and need to be planted where they can't wreak havoc by rooting among choicer small gems such as wood anemones, snowdrops and cyclamen. They often get omitted from gardening books, but we all have these awkward spaces – on steep slopes, between shrubs, on a boundary or close to a wall – and periwinkles fit the bill. There are small-flowered forms: *Vinca minor* f. *alba* 'Gertrude Jekyll' has pure white flowers, and *V. minor* 'La Grave' has azure-blue flowers. Both are lovely, and there is a good purple form too, called 'Atropurpurea'. They flower in late spring, or earlier in mild weather. Despite being more diminutive in scale than the larger *V. major*, all forms of *V. minor* can still overrun you as they can form dense mats of cover.

Most periwinkles tend to flower in late spring, but a few years ago I was given a pink winter-flowering form called *Vinca difformis* 'Jenny Pym', and this is a tremendous plant. Though needing a largish patch – at least 1m (3ft) –

LEFT *Pachysandra terminalis is a good low-growing green for lime-free, rich soil. It will tolerate deep shade, making it useful for problem sites.*

it produces an abundance of green leaf and lots of soft, silver-pink flowers in winter, shining out from beneath a boundary hedge or larger shrub.

IVIES   Rich green can also be provided by ivies, which form a very diverse group. There are hundreds of varieties — some climb, others scramble; some are fast-growing, while others grow very slowly. There is also an immense variety of leaf size and shape, from minuscule to palm-sized and arrow-shaped to crinkled and round.

Our native ivy, *Hedera helix*, has two stages of growth. The juvenile growth has soft, self-clinging stems, but the adult growth is tree-like and bushy at the top. When you see ivy growing in the countryside, you may not realise that the very woody plant at the top of the tree, which has almost-elliptical leaves and boughs, is in fact the same plant as the three-lobed ivy beneath. In a garden setting, however, most ivies only ever produce juvenile foliage as trimming is usually needed to keep them in check (ivy grown up a tree, for example, will need to be cut regularly to prevent it from toppling the supporting tree). The

BELOW *The deeply cut, small leaves of Hedera helix 'Anita' are perfect for softening the edges of a path or container in a shady spot.*

advantage of mature ivy is that it may provide nectar and pollen in late autumn and berries in late winter, something the pollinators and birds will enjoy, and spiders and insects thrive in the shelter too.

Forms of *Hedera helix* are highly useful garden plants as, once established, they can tolerate deep shade and dry conditions. Crinkle-leaved ivies have ruched edges that catch the frost much more effectively than plain-edged varieties. If you grow the wavy-edged 'Parsley Crested', it will happily climb upwards for you, looking vivid and green on mild days and sensational when margined in frost. The best ruched ground-cover ivy that I grow, and that doesn't smother other plants, is the high-glossed 'Ivalace', which makes clumps that span 30–60cm (12–24in). Several 'Ivalace' could be massed together on a slope, or you can mingle it among hardy ferns, particularly polypodiums and polystichums. The small-leaved ivies 'Anita', 'Spetchley' and 'Duckfoot' are all examples of small, non-invasive ivies that are useful for softening the edges of containers, paths, or steps, or growing with other plants.

If you need to remove an unwanted ivy, it can be eradicated by cutting the stems at the base. Once cut, leave the stems where they are for three months, until they die back fully, before removing them. It's far less damaging than trying to pull away the adventitious roots straight away.

LEFT *The leaves of the soft shield fern (Polystichum setiferum) have neat fronds that last all winter.*

FERNS Ferns, like ivies, are best bought from specialist nurseries, as most are not widely available in commercial garden centres. I have found them easy to grow, despite having a dry garden, because I have bought small, young ferns that are eager to establish themselves. Getting to know ferns can be challenging and the forms are many, but they are rewarding if you find the right ones for your garden.

Polypodiums and polystichums both give good winter leaf and will only need tidying in late spring or early summer. In general, polypodiums like good drainage and are best in airy positions, and their leaves are soft to the touch. Polystichums have good spring croziers, which form an S-shape as they unfurl to form leathery fronds. They do well on limy soil, and require good drainage, preferring a slope or a drier site. There are many fine forms of the native soft shield fern, *Polystichum setiferum*, with divided, almost mossy foliage. Most dryopteris, in comparison, become shabby as the weather gets cold. However, if you cut them back in late autumn or early winter you will reveal their brown knuckles – a handsome winter feature. Using bark mulch and wooden logs among your ferns will provide winter protection and an attractive textural backdrop for their feathery foliage.

Golden foliage can look very striking in winter when light levels are low and is ideal for lighting up a dreary corner of the garden. When blending golden or variegated foliage, use a shrub, a ground cover plant, and a taller contrasting grass or perennial, to form a trio of planting. This maximises the effect, as the colour will travel between the tall shrub, the ground and the interesting grass or taller perennial.

golden glimmers

Generally, winter is not the best time for gold-leaved plants – the majority are deciduous, so the leaves don't appear until spring, and most golden foliage becomes duller as the year wears on, reverting to pale green. However, there are some lovely gold-leaved plants that look good at this time of year.

Golden shrubs

BELOW *Choisya ternata 'Sundance' will light up dark corners and will also produce fragrant flowers in late-spring and summer.*

There are a few shrubs with golden evergreen leaves that you can rely on for winter presence. The Mexican orange blossom, *Choisya ternata* 'Sundance', has bright golden yellow foliage; as the season progresses, the leaves turn darker and duller in colour, but they still look gold in winter. There are also variegated elaeagnus that have golden winter leaves. Most named forms of *Elaeagnus pungens* are gold-variegated evergreens; since the majority are fast-growing, they are useful for clothing a boundary fence quickly. The most widely available deep green and gold form is *E. pungens* 'Maculatum'. 'Dicksonii' has green leaves very heavily margined in gold, and 'Frederici' is slower-growing, with pale gold foliage. They will all give you fragrant, silvery white flowers in late autumn, followed by brown fruits that ripen to red. All variegated elaeagnus will grow in shade and can also tolerate salt-laden winds.

Two other groups of plants that can give you golden highlights are conifers and heathers. Winter-flowering heathers, named forms of *Erica carnea*, will thrive on limy soil and make perfect partners

LEFT *Whether you love them or hate them, few plants offer such good winter value as conifers. Jumiper, cryptomeria, chamaecyparis and thuja have been used here to provide an attractive mix of texture and colour.*

for conifers, many of which have handsome new, bright gold growth. The textures combine well, and there is a choice of dwarf conifers that can easily be accommodated in a small garden, for example *Chamaecyparis lawsoniana* 'Springtime', *Juniperus* x *media* 'Old Gold' and *Thuja occidentalis* 'Amber Glow'.

Grass-like golds

At ground level, several grassy plants retain golden foliage. The best of these is *Luzula sylvatica* 'Aurea', a golden woodrush, which will grow in really deep shade. In winter, the floppy, wide-leaved, golden yellow tussocks stand out well against the bare earth, and also look good emerging from leaf litter. The leaves always green up by early summer.

Bowles' golden sedge (*Carex elata* 'Aurea') is a handsome grass that forms a tight clump of erect, narrow leaves that retain their vivid golden colour for most of the winter; each narrow leaf has a green stripe. Bowles' golden grass (*Milium effusum* 'Aureum') has a less neat habit, forming wispy, untidy spiders of leaf against the ground. In winter, it only gives a suggestion of yellow leaf, but is welcome nonetheless. It really comes into its own in spring, when it produces a fine head of shimmering tiny beads in bright chartreuse-yellow. This grass self-seeds, scattering itself around the garden; most seedlings come true from seed.

The most reliably golden winter grass is *Hakonechloa macra*, a Japanese native found naturally on wet, rocky cliffs. It's a floppy grass that spills over the edges of containers and looks best planted alone, although it could be mixed with other plants too. 'All Gold' has pure gold leaves, and 'Aureola' has golden foliage striped in green. There are also forms with silver and white variegations, for example 'Albovariegata'. I have had to grow this in containers, because my soil is just too dry for it to do well.

Another moisture-loving, grass-like winter plant from Japan, found in wet watersides, is *Acorus gramineus*. This low-growing plant forms a horseshoe of grassy leaves that fan out stiffly. There are several named forms. 'Ogon' is the most widely available, with longitudinally striped yellow and green foliage.

Some of the carexes, or sedges, are easier to grow. *Carex oshimensis* 'Evergold' is a selection from another Japanese grass, this time found in dry woods and on rocky slopes, making it less demanding in the garden setting. It's almost like a sea anemone in form, with its slender, narrow leaves that fountain out from a tight waist. Each dark green leaf is liberally striped longitudinally in creamy yellow. This sedge is a stark plant, and looks best drifted through a woodland area, or woven through other plants in the garden, rather than planted on its own or in blocks.

GROWING GOLD   Almost always, golden-leaved plants scorch in bright overhead sun and therefore demand shade. However, there are exceptions. Perversely, the golden ivy, *Hedera helix* 'Buttercup', and golden heucheras – plants that you could utilise in winter as they keep their foliage year round – need full sun in summer to retain their golden, shimmering quality in winter. If planted in shade, their leaves dull when light levels fall. When using golden foliage in the garden, remember that blue, white and even orange flowers look wonderful with golden leaves. However, pink flowers do not. One of my worst gardening mistakes was to plant a blue-pink *Clematis montana* 'Tetrarose' next to the brash yellow ivy *Hedera helix* 'Oro di Bogliasco' (also known as 'Goldheart'). Eventually, faced with the bilious spectacle daily, I had to cull 'Goldheart'.

BELOW Carex 'Evergold' is a low-growing golden grass best used in a ribbon-like fashion in sheltered areas.

Plants with silver-splashed leaves, whether marbled or spotted, are almost sure to be woodlanders, growing naturally under deciduous trees and shrubs. These leaves can take on a snowflake look against bare soil. Snowflake-silvers need a dark background – space them out so they contrast with the soil, surround them with a dressing of bark mulch, or plant them close to tree trunks for contrast.

splashes of silver

Probably my all-time favourite snowflake-effect plant is *Heuchera americana* 'Eco Magnifica', with its silvery scalloped leaves and wine-red veins. In winter, it often acquires a red edge to its leaves too. There are several other silvery varieties, including *H.* 'Pewter Veil', 'Silver Scrolls', 'Can-can' and 'Silver Indiana'. All heucheras tend to like cool conditions, favouring cooler nights, but they also like good drainage and an open, light soil, similar to the

LEFT Brunnera 'Jack Frost' has pewter heart-shaped leaves and tiny cobalt-blue flowers in spring.

conditions found in their native Rocky Mountains. The *Heuchera americana* hybrids are more tolerant of heavier soil than other heucheras.

Heucheras are closely related to tiarellas, and these two genera were crossed to form x *heucherella*. All three genera have good foliage in winter and tiny, dainty, bell-like flowers in early summer. Heucheras are commonly called coral bells and the even daintier x heucherellas are known as foamy bells. The leaves of all three can become ragged in hard winters, but quickly revive as temperatures recover.

As a child, I did well with the older varieties of heuchera in a north-facing suburban garden, where I grew them on a slope out of sun. Then, heucheras were mainly forms of *Heuchera sanguinea* and were grown primarily for their summer flower sprays, which were often coral-red or pink. In winter, they also provided soft green leaf. Today, most heucheras are bred with foliage in mind. There are green varieties, marbled and speckled with silver, as well as golden, red and purple forms.

The main problem with heucheras is vine weevil attack. I think this tends to happen because as plants age they produce brittle, lax stems that expose an open crown, allowing the adult weevils free access. Regularly adding humus-rich compost around these stems keeps the crown more solid, or you can dig up the original plant and pot up pieces of stem in gritty compost in late summer or early autumn. It's vital to divide heucheras and x heucherellas every other year to avoid these lax stems and keep them in good heart. If you've a cool, shady garden, these lovely plants are well worth pursuing.

The leaf rosettes of the common foxglove, *Digitalis purpurea*, are silver-green, almost downy, as are the leaves of several verbascums. These biennials provide a good rosette of greener leaf before flowering in their second year, and provide useful shelter for insects. *D. purpurea* will happily survive shade, while verbascums prefer an open, sunny site.

Pulmonarias are perennial, but they flower early in the year and many varieties – particularly the dappled ones – have good winter leaf. One of the best spotted varieties is the aptly named *Pulmonaria saccharata* 'Leopard', with silver markings on the dark green leaves and brick-red flowers from late winter to late spring. This cultivar endures for years. Not all forms of *P. saccharata* are as hardy, for example 'Dora Bielefeld', which suffers in very cold weather.

The two best plain silver-leaved pulmonarias are 'Majesté' and 'Diana Clare', which both flower in early spring. 'Majesté' has white-silvered leaves and pale pink and blue flowers, while 'Diana Clare' has metallic, silver-green foliage and richer, violet-blue flowers with a hint of purple. Both are fine varieties that are unusual in keeping their silver shading throughout winter.

The same frosted-silver-against-the-ground effect can be achieved with the pretty white-flowered deadnettle *Lamium maculatum* 'White Nancy'. This low-growing, gentle spreader has silvered leaves edged in a fine green edge. It has the best foliage of all deadnettles and is not invasive. Trim back this lamium in late summer to keep a compact plant for winter effect. (Avoid the similar sounding *Lamium galeobdolon*, it's a silver and green variegated dead-nettle with yellow flowers and is highly invasive.) Some lesser celandines (*Ranunculus ficaria*) have brilliant foliage too, making a contribution from midwinter on. 'Brambling' and 'Randall's White' have silver veins in their kidney-shaped leaves.

Both autumn-flowering *Cyclamen hederifolium* and spring-flowering *C. coum* can also give you lovely silver foliage in winter, either plain-frosted, veined or marbled. *C. hederifolium* produces flowers before it produces leaf. The flowers often appear in late summer, following a night of rain, and seem to spring as if from nowhere; a few weeks later the leaves appear and last all winter. *C. coum* does it the other way round. The dainty, kidney-shaped leaves appear in late autumn and then the short flowers, always nosed in magenta, open in midwinter.

ABOVE *The spear-shaped leaves of* Arum italicum *subsp.* italicum '*Marmoratum*' *appear in late autumn and then disappear in late spring.*

There is another important difference between the two cyclamen. *Cyclamen hederifolium* is long-lived and makes huge corms, which after only five years can reach the size of dinner plates and can eventually become as large as dustbin lids. I've seen this for myself in the wood at Bitton in Gloucestershire, planted up by Canon Ellacombe (1822–1916), author of *In a Gloucestershire Garden* (published in 1895). They remain like huge relics partly above the ground. The corms of spring-flowering *C. coum,* however, rarely exceed 8cm (3in) in diameter, and the plant is short-lived. *C. coum* is diminutive enough to mix well with snowdrops and other early woodlanders, whereas if you plant *C. hederifolium* beside these tiny harbingers of spring the dustbin lid will soon flatten the walnut. Like a fat man nudging up to a dainty girl on a train, it's not a happy situation; you need to segregate them. Ants like to carry the sticky sweet seeds of both away and they lick the coating off and then discard the seeds – so cyclamen wander!

Arum italicum also seems to wander and spread rather mysteriously. For this reason, it may be too invasive for your garden, but the leaves unfurl as fresh as can be in late autumn, that most lacklustre of seasons. The leaves are gloriously handsome, often marbled arrowheads, and they will happily spring up close to the trunks of trees. *Arum italicum* subsp. *italicum* 'Marmoratum' (still mainly sold under its old, simpler name of 'Pictum') has very marbled leaves.

Dark-leaved plants add depth, richness and drama to a scheme. I remember a friend struggling with a border of peach and apricot flowers, and it just didn't please the eye until she added red and dark foliage, using dahlias, cotinus and sambucus. Those dark touches brought the whole to life. Use dark plants with contrasting or paler colours, but use them sparingly as they can be sombre.

dark, dramatic foliage

BELOW *Black strappy Ophiopogon planiscapus 'Nigrescens' is an indispensable low-growing addition.*

In winter, as with gold foliage, many dark-leaved plants are not available. However, the grass-like, low-growing *Ophiopogon planiscapus* 'Nigrescens' looks its best in winter. In my garden it grows in gravel, where it forms a striking contrast with the silvery phlomis (*Phlomis italica*) that grows nearby. It also creeps its way beneath several climbers growing against the wall, in shade. It can be mass-planted under contrasting red dogwood stems, and

forms a perfect carpet under silver-stemmed rubus. Wherever you plant black ophiopogon, it prefers a warm site. If happy, it will also produce pink flower spikes followed by violet berries, especially in sunny summers. It spreads, although non-aggressively, so every year I dig some up in early autumn and plant it in outdoor containers to add drama to red cyclamen, miniature yellow daffodils or blue hyacinths.

There are also several wispy brown sedges (*Carex*) – not as dramatic as black ophiopogon, but they provide useful swirls of filament leaf, in shades of rust- to olive-brown, in open, airy positions. *Carex comans* bronze form, *C. flagellifera* and *C. testacea* are all from New Zealand and will provide an arching winter fountain of soft copper-brown in winter. When underplanted with blue *Anemone blanda*, they shine in spring too. In fact, I used to be teased by friends because my favourite plant was a cascading *C. testacea*, with its long stems topped by seedheads. I allowed it to drift over the gravel like a mother hen with chicks – to them it looked dead, but its gentle sway saw me through many a winter.

Purple-leaved heucheras can also be used successfully in winter. 'Palace Purple' made a splash on the horticultural scene in the 1980s because it swung the pendulum away from heuchera flower to heuchera leaf. In 1991 it was voted Perennial Plant of the Year, and was named after the palace at Kew where it began life. 'Palace Purple' grows best in shade, as the colours seem more lustrous, but it is also happy in sun if given good soil. It keeps its colour well all year, and looks lovely on woodland edges close to silver-leaved pulmonarias.

In recent years, 'Palace Purple' has been superseded by 'Plum Pudding', which is an even better dark heuchera with plum-purple leaves and a tight growth habit. Then there are those with ruffled leaves, such as the lovely 'Chocolate Ruffles'. The upper surfaces are a dusky chocolate and the under-sides a blue-purple. 'Purple Petticoats' is also one of the best. It has deep purple foliage with frilled edges, and it is reputedly tougher than the others too. Most of the heucheras with superb winter foliage have very poor flowers – you can't have it all; I usually snip mine off.

Heucheras are members of the Saxifragaceae, as are bergenias. And if you compare their flowerheads, the substantial bells of bergenias do resemble those of heuchera, only they are larger. Commonly known as elephants' ears, bergenias are so named because of their large leaves, and many are bred to have reddened foliage in winter. *Bergenia* 'Bressingham Ruby' was named for its foliage rather than flower colour, and the leaves keep their colour for most of the year. 'Abendglut' also colours well. 'Eric Smith', which is harder to find, has crinkled leaves with bronze upper sides and a darker, redder underside. The straight species *B. purpurascens* probably plays some part in them all. Its leaves colour up to beetroot-red.

I have never done well with bergenias because I have always owned south-facing gardens and they seem to like cool roots. My neighbour, who has an east-facing garden where thugs battle it out, triumphs with them year after year. Although there's more leaf than flower, the foliage is handsome in winter. In all, bergenias are most useful in sheltered positions where they can remain undisturbed. This may also avoid the problem of their flowers being decimated by frost too, a common problem in some areas.

Pittosporum tenuifolium 'Purpureum', a columnar shrub, has wonderful, almost black crinkled foliage. The superior 'Tom Thumb' has even darker foliage, a more compact habit and forms a rounded mound. You do need mild winters, a sheltered site and good drainage to grow pittosporums.

There are several attractive dark phormiums that could be grown in the ground, if given good drainage. *Phormium* 'Platt's Black' is very dark, and there are many New Zealand-bred cultivars that are finding their way into Britain. Like all New Zealanders, high light levels and an open position are essential.

The small evergreen shrub with shiny leaves, *Photinia x fraseri* 'Red Robin', has bronze to bright red new shoots; some years, the leaves will retain their red colour into winter. This is a highly useful shrub, but its overexposure in garden centres has put some gardeners off. I also admire the evergreen

RIGHT *There are countless heucheras from the sultry 'Plum Pudding', shown here, to the silvered 'Eco Magnifolia'.*

Viburnum x *hillieri* 'Winton', which has oval green leaves that turn bronze-red in winter and produces creamy white flowers in early summer, once it has reached a few years old. In the winter, this handsome shrub stands out at the back of the border, and in the summer it provides a good, leafy background for herbaceous perennials, such as hardy geraniums.

hips, haws and berries

4

Silver-dusted winter mornings have a cool, stark kind of beauty, but they are so much more spectacular when there are colourful touches of clear red studding the garden. In fact, a touch of red in any border, whatever the season, seems to add clarity and definition to a planting scheme and enhance its appeal.

touches of red

The 'touch of red principle' is something many artists employ in their paintings. When I was studying art at school, I can clearly remember my art mistress explaining that every great painting had at least one tiny touch of red to 'bring every other colour to life'. An example that illustrates this is an anecdote I once heard about the watercolourist J.M.W. Turner (1775–1851), who was most famous for his shipwrecks and seascapes. He was apparently exhibiting a picture in a competition, and visitors were asked to vote for their favourite. Turner's painting was lagging in support, and so he went to the gallery and spent several hours gazing at his painting, trying to analyse why it was less popular with the public than the works of his rivals. Finally, he took out a fine brush and a small pot of red paint and deftly added a tiny red buoy to the foreground, completing the task in less than a minute. By the end of the competition, Turner's painting had won: that extra touch of red had made all the difference. The same device is employed again in Turner's picture of Venice, *Giudecca, La Donna della Salute and San Giorgio*, painted in 1840. The wide canal, lined by Venetian palaces and churches, is a sea green and blue mixture of subtle colours, but in the foreground, one of the small sailors or bargees has bright red trousers: another tiny speck of red.

In the same way, red is the touch-paper colour in our gardens, keeping the flame of hope burning during winter. Generally, it is the berries, hips or haws that provide that much-needed glint of red or orange. It is worth remembering that there are many shades of orange and red berry and that their impact changes according to the setting. The most vibrant combination is bright-green leaf against clear red fruit and any scheme involving these two colours, which lie on opposite sides of the colour wheel, needs a supporting chorus of green leaf to keep the theme going. If the berries, fruits or hips stud bare branches, try to use the sky as a backdrop or plant them in grass – for when those fruits land on the grassy green they'll provide the same clear contrast.

ABOVE *Employ the 'touch of red' principle to bring the garden to life with a dash of colour.*

RIGHT *Wild rosehips rimed in frost remind us that it's the single-flowered species roses that tend to produce hips.*

PREVIOUS PAGES *There are over a hundred types of cotoneaster. Many berry well and shine in winter sun.*

As a gardener, I'm perpetually torn between feeding the birds and creating a winter spectacle. Should I plant unpalatable, berrying trees and shrubs that I know the birds will avoid? Or should I applaud as the luscious fruits disappear, gorged upon by that marauding trio of berry-stealers – the fieldfares, blackbirds and starlings? On balance, I admire the athletic leaps and bounds required by these cumbersome birds, and I enjoy seeing them gobbling up the berries.

Plants that produce hips, berries and haws tend to take up quite a bit of space, because you're allowing them to flower and set fruit. In a small, modern garden, it is vital to choose a compact plant rather than trying to restrict the growth of a rapidly expanding giant by attacking it with secateurs each spring. All plants must have enough space to shine and develop. Overplanting is a mistake in any garden: all shrubs and trees become distorted in shape when hemmed in by a jungle of encroaching foliage.

Many shrubs are studded with jewelled clusters of berries in winter, offset by a backdrop of evergreen leaves. Hollies are the most obvious choice, but pyracanthas and cotoneaster will also provide you with a feast of colourful red, orange or yellow fruit.

berrying shrubs

Pyracanthas, or firethorns, can look very handsome trained up against a wall or fence. They have the advantage of growing happily against north-facing walls, are evergreen, and produce colourful red, orange or yellow berries that last into winter. On the debit side, many pyracanthas suffer from fireblight (*Erwinia amylovora*), a debilitating bacterial disease that causes dieback in members of the rose family (the Rosaceae). It can affect apples, pears, and other related shrubs. You can usually prune out infected stems, but do sterilise your secateurs afterwards – a good, hot, soapy wash is my solution. To avoid fireblight, it is well worth using disease-resistant varieties – so think Native American, and seek out 'Mohave' (bright orange), 'Shawnee' (yellow to light orange) or 'Navajo' (orange-red). The weeping shrub *Pyracantha* Alexander Pendula ('RENOLEX') is another good form, with cascading clusters of orange-red fruit.

Cotoneasters are also good for winter berries. Although I find many rather uninspiring, there are several I do admire. *Cotoneaster lacteus* is a lovely evergreen shrub, with large, oval, leathery leaves – the upper sides are a deep sage to olive green, and the undersides are pale grey and felted. This contrast between the dark upper side and pale lower leaf shows itself as a thin margin around the leaf edge when viewed from the side, adding neat definition. The red fruits, although small, are borne in wide clusters and look stunning against the thick, substantial leaves. The fruits have the added advantage of not ripening until late in the year and they persist into midwinter and beyond. *C. lacteus* is about 3–4m (10–13ft) high, and is useful for a boundary edge or as a specimen in large lawn.

The tree-like evergreen *Cotoneaster frigidus* 'Cornubia' needs even more space, reaching 6m (20ft) tall. But it provides

BELOW Pyracantha *berries usually last for the first half of winter before the blackbirds gobble them up.*

ABOVE Cotoneaster frigidis *'Cornubia'* is a spectacular, berry-laden, tall cotoneaster suitable for larger gardens. It forms a large shrub, or can be trained into a standard to make an attractive small tree.

an enormous number of bright red berries, and the branches are often weighed down with the bounty. For some reason, the birds seem to shun them.

Another I really rate is the semi-evergreen *Cotoneaster* 'Hybridus Pendulus'. This cotoneaster has lengthy, prostrate branches covered in long, narrow, shiny leaves, and it can be bought either as a shrub or as a standard, reaching about 1.5–2m (5–6ft) high. If you opt for a standard, you tend to get a small weeping tree. The advantage is that grafted standards are less prone to the bacterial disease fireblight, presumably because the rootstock below the graft is fireblight-resistant. The round, bright red, marble-like fruits make an excellent autumn feature and often extend into winter. They have that appealing way of shedding their fruit on the floor beneath. If the berries land on grass, the combination of green grass and red makes both colours appear more vibrant.

The Winter Garden at Cambridge University Botanic Garden is good for inspiration. There are three choice cotoneasters here: *Cotoneaster conspicuus*, a medium-sized shrub with orange-red fruit; *C. microphyllus* 'Highlight', a stiffly branched evergreen with tiny leaves and reddish pink berries; and *C. salicifolius* 'Herbstfeuer', syn. 'Autumn Fire', a lax, wide-spreading, semi-evergreen shrub with bright green pointed leaves and vivid orange-red clusters of red berries.

Spiny winter warmers

The best berrying shrubs, the hollies, come in many sizes and forms, and grow slowly, so are often ideal for smaller gardens. Most varieties grown in the garden are evergreen. Do bear in mind that hollies are dioecious, which means 'two houses' in Latin and refers to the fact that the male and female flowers are, in most cases, on separate plants. In order to produce berries, pollen usually has to pass between the pair, so you tend to need at least two hollies to produce fruit. I can imagine many of you saying 'I've only got one holly and yet I get berries', but most probably you've only got berries because there are other hollies close by, either in neighbouring gardens or in nearby lanes or woodland.

If you're planting hollies for their berries, you need to allow your plant free rein to flower and set fruit, so smart topiarising is really out. You will also have to search out good free-fruiting females, while planting some males as pollinators too. Generally, a ratio of one male to five females will give lots of berries. To find out whether a holly is male or female, look up the variety in a reliable book, or consult a nursery. You'll need this information once you realise that 'Golden King' is a female and 'Silver Queen' is a male – you can't go by name alone.

The hollies described below are generally available at most garden centres, but should you wish to grow lots of varieties, do visit a specialist nursery, where you will find a vast range that you rarely see elsewhere.

NATIVE HOLLIES Britain's native holly, *Ilex aquifolium*, takes its species name from *aquila* (meaning eagle), giving you a helpful hint that the spiny leaves resemble eagles' talons in their sharpness. These are savage on the fingers, and even more dangerous to the eyes, so it's advisable never to plant this prickly holly in a herbaceous border or another area of the garden that needs continual attention. Instead, use forms of *I. aquifolium* as boundary plants on the outer edges, or as specimens in lawns, or among other shrubs.

I'd recommend the following female variegated forms of *Ilex aquifolium* for berrying: 'Handsworth New Silver' has mottled, greyish green leaves thinly edged with a regular margin of custard-cream yellow. This holly always looks extremely sleek and crisp, forming a rounded bush. The leaves are long and slender, on dark stems, and it bears abundant red berries. 'Argentea Marginata' forms a columnar shape, and each green leaf is edged in a white margin. There are subtle splashes and overlaps on the leaves too. There is also a pendulous form, 'Argentea Marginata Pendula', which makes an excellent specimen set in grass. 'Madame Briot' is brasher, with rich green leaves that are mottled and margined in vivid gold. This prickly, strong holly forms a large shrub before maturing into a small tree. 'Golden Milkboy' is a good male for pollination.

All variegated hollies are good at lighting up dark corners. After all, hollies are understorey plants, usually found under mighty oaks in the countryside, and are therefore adapted to shady positions. When planting hollies, experience has taught me that it's always best to start with a young, small specimen rather than trying to introduce an expensive mature holly. Hollies resent disturbance,

RIGHT *The weeping golden-variegated holly* Ilex aquifolium *'Argentea Marginata Pendula' carries many berries, given a male partner.*

and even young, newly planted specimens tend to sit still for a couple of years or longer before taking off. Hollies are rather like people in growth pattern – when young, they are rakishly slender, but they invariably fill out when mature. Variegated hollies have a tendency to produce green shoots, and these should be removed as soon as they appear to prevent the whole plant reverting to green.

Although variegated hollies are lovely, you should never underestimate the value of a green-leaved holly with red berries. The conical 'Pyramidalis' is often grown commercially, and is popular because of its less spiny leaves and heavy clusters of berries positioned close to the outer shoots. 'J.C. van Tol' has shiny, almost spineless green leaves and clusters of berries borne along the stems. It is useful in small gardens, as it is self-fertile and doesn't need a male to set berries. 'Pyramidalis' can also produce berries on its own.

ROUNDER-LEAVED HOLLIES The 18th-century passion for orangeries full of tender plants led to the cultivation of *Ilex perado* – a large-leaved green holly, with huge berries, from the Azores. In winter this lovely plant stayed indoors, in enormous containers, but in summer these large pots were wheeled outdoors to decorate the outside of the orangery. Bees inevitably fed on the flowers of this exotic holly, picking up a hairdo full of pollen before visiting the native hollies nearby. Berries were formed from the new accidental crosses, these were then ingested by birds, and later hit the ground with the droppings. As a result of all this, new hybrid hollies appeared, providing us with a hardy, rounder-leaved holly that tends to have larger but fewer berries than our native hollies. John Claudius Loudon (1783–1843), landscape architect, writer and a

Victorian authority on shrubs and trees, named the new hybrid *Ilex x altaclerensis* (literally translated as 'House of Clere') to reflect the name of the estate where the first hybrids were identified in 1838 – Highclere Castle near Newbury.

These crosses have resulted in some fine varieties. Their leaf shape varies from round to elliptical, and the leaves are much less spiny than the native species; as a result, these hollies can be used at the back of the herbaceous border, as single specimens or as a hedge. Alternating a variegated form with a plain green one makes an attractive textured backdrop for other plants.

Ilex x altaclerensis 'Belgica Aurea' is an upright, handsome female holly with lance-shaped green leaves edged in yellow; however, it does not bear many berries. 'Golden King', a female with very round green leaves with wide, irregular gold margins, produces more berries but has a tendency to revert to plain green leaves. 'Lawsoniana' is another female with rounded, rich green leaves splashed in golden yellow. Where the yellow overlaps the dark green, a third shade of bright green appears, but berries are few and far between. 'Camelliifolia' has a stunning conical shape and attractive deep green leaves, but again berrying can be sparse.

Finally, it's worth making room for *Ilex x meserveae* 'Blue Prince'. Known as the blue holly because of its blue stems, or the New York holly after the place where it was raised, this form will provide an abundant supply of male pollen to promote good berrying among your chosen harem of fruiting *I. aquifolium* and *I. x altaclerensis* females.

ABOVE Ilex x altaclerensis *'Golden King' has round leaves randomly edged in golden yellow – though the berries are sometimes in short supply.*

Every garden should contain one ornamental tree with hanging clusters of berries or fruit in a warm red or strong orange. You'll create a spectacle and please the birds too. The hawthorns are under-appreciated by many gardeners and these accommodating trees are capable of growing in towns and cities regardless of soil.

fiery fruiting trees

BELOW *The round haws of Crataegus prunifolia stud the bare branches.*

There are three groups of small trees that you could draw upon to add fiery touches of red or orange to your garden. First, the hawthorns (*Crataegus*), which are more than just lovely spring-flowering trees. In fact, my favourite small tree of all time is the oriental thorn, *Crataegus orientalis*. Once called the cut-leaved hawthorn (*C. laciniata*), *Crataegus orientalis* has neat, grey-green leaves with finely cut edges. In spring, the creamy cake-scented blossom is flecked with scarlet anthers and then the large round haws form by early autumn. These have the same speckled, mellow colouring as a ripe Cox's Orange Pippin in miniature. I must admit that by mid- to late autumn these haws have generally disappeared down a blackbird's gullet.

There are several dark, glossy-leaved varieties with red haws that emerge later and therefore stay on the tree for longer. One notable example is *Crataegus* x *lavalleei* 'Carrierei', also known as Carrière's hybrid thorn, although the thorns are few and far between. It produces orange-red fruits that show up against the leaves well into late autumn. If the leaves drop late in the year, the fruits on this small, dense tree stay on into winter.

Crataegus crus-galli, the cockspur thorn, is a small North American tree that bears clusters of red haws above rounded green leaves. The finest thorn for winter fruit, though, is *C. prunifolia*, which is similar to and has probably derived from *C. crus-galli* and has shiny, leathery leaves and large, round fruits studded along the branches. Both of these are

compact, broad-headed trees that colour well in late autumn. I once saw a formal grid of nine beautiful *C. prunifolia* trees planted over ferns, reaching out to form an overhead canopy of flat-stretched branches. As the leaves fell, the fruits stayed clinging to the bare branches as effectively as a string of fairy lights. The drawback of both *C. crus-galli* and *C. prunifolia* is that they have downward-facing thorns; although sparse, they are wounding.

Hawthorns have another major advantage – they are accommodating in poor soil and harsh situations, even surviving in polluted air.

Crab apples are also great trees for winter fruits. When it comes to selecting varieties, one red-fruiting form stands supreme – *Malus* x *robusta* 'Red Sentinel'. The abundant bright red fruits, which follow white spring flowers, are studded in clusters along the branches and persist well into winter. A great advantage of this tree is that it doesn't suffer from scab, a scourge of many other crab apples.

Finally, the sorbus – a genus full of small-berrying trees in many shades, including red. With their finely divided leaves, autumn colour, numerous flowers and berries and slow growth habit, it's not surprising that they are among the top three trees for the garden (the other two being cherries and crab apples). *Sorbus sargentiana*, collected by English plant hunter Ernest Wilson from China in 1908, is a choice tree. It reaches 9m (28ft), so is good for small gardens, and it bears stunning, large, rounded heads of red berries that measure up to 15cm (6in) across and remain on the tree all winter. It also has red sticky buds in spring, and in good years the autumn foliage matures to bright scarlet. Generally, the meaty smell of the flowers (designed to attract pollinating flies) puts me off sorbus, but the abundance of fruit makes *S. sargentiana* really worth having.

LEFT *Crab apple* Malus x robusta *'Red Sentinel' is another fiery beacon for the winter garden.*

RIGHT *The red-berried* Sorbus sargentiana *is one of the finest winter warmers.*

Bright, glossy rosehips also add much-needed glimmers of winter red to our gardens, and look particularly stunning when surrounded by angular, ice-crystal edging. When considering winter hips, the roses that make the best ones tend to be large shrub roses with single or loose semi-double flowers.

tempting rosehips

Some roses, for example the rugosas, produce hips early. In fact, I dug up *Rosa* 'Fru Dagmar Hastrup' purely because she set globular, pale orange hips in midsummer. They used to make me shudder and bring autumn threateningly close before I was ready to embrace it. Her hips disintegrated well before winter too, and finally she had to go.

Large shrub roses need plenty of space around them in order to show their elegant, arching branches, laden with hips, to best effect. The branches need space to throw out their shoots and to develop their distinctive silhouettes. If you prune and restrict the growth of these large, airy roses, it both destroys their shape and removes their ability to set hips. For this reason, combined with the fact that the branches can be thorny, they are best avoided in small gardens. Most hips will have to be pruned away in late winter if they haven't been eaten by then, but at least you will have enjoyed their hips from autumn to midwinter.

LARGE SHRUB ROSES *Rosa moyesii*, a species rose from western China, has beautiful, flagon-shaped hips that stay on through winter as well as vibrant summer flowers, but it is a tall, sparse rose. However, there are selected forms that make excellent garden plants. 'Geranium' (raised at RHS Wisley in 1938) is more compact, reaching just 2–2.2m (6–7ft), and has better foliage too. The blazing red single flowers are followed by glossy, bright sealing-wax-red flagons, which will bring a splash of colour to the back of a border. 'Highdownensis', a seedling of *R. moyesii* raised by Sir Frederick Stern of Highdown in Sussex, c.1928,

BELOW *The flagon-shaped hips of Rosa sweginzowii provide vibrant splashes of red.*

RIGHT Rosa moyesii *is an*
easy rose to accommodate at
the rear of a perennial border.

is larger than 'Geranium', reaching about 3m (10ft) high and across. Its cerise-crimson flowers are followed by orange-red hips. The more compact and graceful 'Hillieri', a cross between *R. moyesii* and *R. macrophylla*, has single pink flowers, large, orange-red flagons, and reaches 2.5 x 2.2m (8 x 7ft).

Rosa davidii bears clusters of late mallow-pink flowers that are followed by bunches of small scarlet flagons. Other flagon-hipped roses include *R. sweginzowii*, *R. setipoda* and *R. macrophylla*. 'Master Hugh' is a particularly fine form of the latter. The sweet briar (*R. rubiginosa*, syn. *R. eglanteria*), with its apple-scented foliage, clear pink flowers and masses of oval red hips, is lovely in a large garden. *R. multibracteata* is a graceful shrub rose, with fern-like leaves and rose-lilac single flowers, followed by small red hips covered in bristles. All these roses shine from late summer until early winter. However, they make large, rather gaunt shrubs, about 2.2m (7ft) high, and so require plenty of space.

Slightly smaller is *Rosa woodsii*, a North American species rose, reaching 1.5m (5ft), with lilac-pink flowers followed by sealing-wax-red hips that last into winter.

One species rose I would always find room for, even in a small garden, is the grey-leaved *Rosa glauca*. In hot weather, the foliage reddens, and although it is a large, open shrub rose if left unpruned, it has wonderful hips from late summer until midwinter. The long, slender flagons are held in downward-facing clusters, and they are a rich brown-pink, the colour of rich cocoa, in late summer. Later, they turn a dull brown-orange, mahogany colour, and every seed-

eating bird in the area visits them. The flowers are small, single and pink. As they are not particularly attractive, I cut this rose back to the base every year to encourage stronger stems and larger leaves at the expense of the flowers. In hot summers, the dark foliage becomes even more intense.

CLIMBERS AND RAMBLERS Luckily, some roses bred for their flowers will leave you with hips by default. A white rambler of mine, which I believe to be 'Wedding Day', spans the gate with the soft apricot 'Goldfinch', an almost thornless rambler. In autumn, 'Wedding Day' bears small clusters of brown-red hips that stay on over winter, forming a beautiful garland. These hips must be unpalatable to birds, as they remain untouched until I prune them out.

ABOVE *The hips of some roses are flushed with shades of warm yellow and orange, providing a lovely glow.*

The giant 'Kiftsgate' also has very pretty clusters of red hips, and is often cited as worth growing for that very reason. However, you would need a pair of binoculars to focus on them, as it climbs high up into the trees and the hips soon disappear out of sight. 'Kiftsgate' is extremely vigorous, and it is charged with killing six mature beech trees at the Cotswold garden it is named after.

Other ramblers or climbers with excellent hips include 'Kew Rambler', which has bright pink single flowers and is very vigorous, and 'Francis E. Lester', a scented, clear apple-blossom pink rose with bosses of yellow stamens. 'Rambling Rector' is a rather prickly, large white rambler, and 'Madame Grégoire Staechelin' is a once-flowering pink climbing rose that is grown for its sweet-pea fragrance. 'Cupid' has light peach-pink flowers, between single and semi-double, with visible yellow stamens, and bears large, long-lasting, round orange-red hips.

HYBRID MUSKS The Hybrid Musk roses, which generally produce clusters of bloom from late summer onwards, are among the best roses for hips. They're a variable bunch, but they were all selected by the English rosarian Reverend Joseph Pemberton, primarily for their scent. His trio of ladies, bred in the 1920s, are among the best roses ever bred: 'Penelope' has semi-double, salmon-orange flowers that open and fade to cream-pink and are followed by small, round, coral-pink hips; the warm apricot-pink 'Felicia' and copper-apricot 'Cornelia' will also produce some hips, although not as effectively or as beautifully as 'Penelope'. The larger, more open bright red 'Wilhelm' produces round orange-red hips ringed by pale chalices, and 'Will Scarlet' (a sport of 'Wilhelm') also has these same glossy hips.

'Bonica', although not a hybrid musk, is one of the prettiest garden roses. It is low-growing, 1.2m (4ft) high at the most, and its fragrant, clear pink flowers always produce some small, dainty hips. It does well on poor soil.

Berrying plants

FRUIT SET, WHETHER IT'S BERRY, HIP OR HAW, IS ALWAYS MORE SUCCESSFUL when the plant is grown in a warm position in some sunshine, because pollinating insects prefer to work in the sun. Generally, a mild spring and warm summer tends to mean more berries.

Pruning berrying plants

The pruning of berrying shrubs should be carried out after the berries have disintegrated or disappeared into the beaks of hungry birds, in late winter or early spring. However, they must never be pruned after bud break, when the sap is rising. You can pick the stems of berrying hollies in early winter, before the birds get hold of them, and put them in water in a cool place. They will last for weeks, and make ideal Christmas decorations.

Growing roses

When planting roses of any kind, bare-root roses are best. Order them in summer and plant them in winter. Unpack your roses as soon as they arrive. If the ground is unfrozen, you can plant them straight away. Otherwise, place them in a cool, frost-free place (for example a shed or garage) for no longer than a week. If the ground remains hard, you may have to heel them in temporarily. To do this, dig a trench with one slanting side at an angle of about 45 degrees, lay each rose at an angle, and space the roses well in the trench. Gently cover the roots and firm them.

Planting roses

As soon as the weather allows, plant them properly. Dig a large enough hole to allow you to spread the roots out, and throw a handful of bone meal into the hole and mix it in with the soil. Shorten any really long roots to 15–30cm (6–12in), place the rose in the hole and cover the roots with soil, making sure the union (the bumpy part at the bottom of the rose) is 2.5cm (1in) below the soil surface. Press the soil down firmly with your feet and water well.

Finally, cut all newly planted roses back hard to allow new, sturdy shoots to form from the base of the rose. This gives the rose stability in two ways: the energy goes into producing roots, rather than sending sap up the stems, and it also prevents wind-rock

(which disturbs unrooted and newly planted specimens). Reduce each stem to 7–12cm (3–5in) in length, to an outward-facing bud. In subsequent years, pruning will differ according to the type of rose.

Pruning roses

LARGE SHRUB ROSES Large shrub roses grown mainly for their hips need pruning in late winter. Remove the three Ds – the diseased, the dying, and the dead branches, to form an open, branching shape. This may involve removing one or two of the older stems from the base. Then all you need to do is to reduce the flowering wands by one-third. Cutting shoots back hard on roses only applies with Hybrid Teas – any shrub rose is pruned in this gentle 'third-back' style.

PRUNING RAMBLERS Ramblers mostly flower once and they usually produce strong, new growth in summer. In late autumn or early winter, take out two or three of the old stems from the base and tie in any new, strong shoots. At this stage the new wood is still supple, and easy to bend and train. By midwinter, it has become much harder.

PRUNING CLIMBERS Climbers are repeat-flowering and they are often much less vigorous than ramblers. In late autumn or winter, shorten the long leading shoots by one-third and then shorten and tidy the lateral shoots. Never cut a climbing rose hard back, or it may never recover.

HYBRID MUSKS These are also pruned sympathetically in late autumn and winter. Keep the shape, but cut back firmly to a strong outer shoot towards the top of each stem. Use a slanting cut going away from the bud.

structural features

5

Winter tends to pick up and highlight inanimate garden detail: the hard landscape of a path or terrace, the necessary garden shed and outbuildings, and the large expanse of fence or wall are all at their most noticeable now that the garden is in retreat.

the hard landscape

If you're lucky enough to enjoy a dusting of snow, or an ice-rimming hoar frost, it will pick out every pleasing contour. But if your garden structure isn't very well considered, it will also show up the mistakes. Winter is therefore an excellent time to evaluate your hard structure and act on the

imperfections, while gardening tasks are at a minimum.

The style of your house and the garden's surroundings will determine the style of your hard landscape. If the house has classic square lines and straight walls, you need equally strong lines for paths and terraced areas. Conversely, a small country cottage could accommodate a series of casual paths weaving through cottage-style planting. So examine your garden setting, and try to complement the character and style of your home and surrounding scenery.

If there's landscape beyond your garden, don't truncate it by adding a hedge; instead, try to lead the garden into it imaginatively. A far-off wood on a hill could be mimicked by cloud-trained box or yew roundels set on man-made miniature hills, thereby linking the garden with the distant scenery. If privacy is a priority, you could create glimpses of the far beyond by creating windows or gaps in your hedge. Even a tiny window, carefully placed, will give a glimpse of the scenery beyond, while providing privacy at the same time.

If you're lucky enough to have a meandering river, canal or other waterway running through your garden, it will demand equally flowing, snaking borders close by. Ideally, try to create a link between your garden and the view beyond:

LEFT *A simple curved bridge over a small stream finishes off this area at Arrow Cottage in Herefordshire.*

PREVIOUS PAGES *A dusting of snow and frost highlights the structural lines of the topiary and hedging, steps and summerhouse at Hazelbury manor gardens, Wiltshire.*

ABOVE *A textured path, lost in summer, shows its every hump and bump in low winter light.*

if there are willows on a far bank, echo the view with a planting of lacquered stems in warm colours. The taller *Salix alba* var. *vitellina* 'Britzensis', the scarlet willow, will send up slender, orange-red stems that reach 2.5m (8ft) in height. If you plant the shorter *Cornus sanguinea* 'Winter Beauty', a compact bush of red, yellow and orange shoots, at the forefront you have a branching sea of warm colours to blend with a reflection of twigs from the trees on the far side.

Material matters

Winter is a good time to think about your garden's layout. If you decide to add or change any hard surfaces, select your materials carefully, always opting for the highest quality you can afford on the basis of durability. Perhaps the most important thing of all when it comes to hard landscape is to tone the materials in with your local soil and building materials (which tend to match the soil) so they complement each other. The best way to achieve this is to source products locally rather than from a nationwide chain outlet. Ask your local builder, check local quarries or gravel pits, and check out any landscaping suppliers. However, if this proves too difficult or expensive, it makes good sense to take a sample of your garden soil in a sealed polythene bag to the garden centre or builders' merchants, in order to check for colour matches and clashes. We always assume that soil is brown, but the spectrum ranges from almost black to henna red, through to pale sand.

Where I live in the Cotswolds, the natural geology varies from golden honey-coloured stone at the northern end of the range to an almost porridge-grey towards the south. Despite this marked difference, both colours could be labelled 'Cotswold' in the shops, so never make assumptions based on the product name. Adding the wrong shade of stone or gravel will really stand out as a mistake in winter.

When selecting materials, make sure you choose the right surface for the job. For example, gun-metal-grey slate will set off an alpine bed of low-growing, toning silver plants beautifully, but it isn't suitable for a well-used path, as it

will shatter into pieces. Similarly, some stones can become very slippery in the winter wet and are unsuitable for paths or paved areas that you will have to traverse regularly. A swathe of pebbles or gravel may be an effective way of structuring or decorating a small garden, but may be impractical for a larger site. Generally, for a main path or terrace, paviors or wooden decking are better than loose materials, such as gravel or slate.

GRAVEL, SLATE AND PEBBLES Gravel works particularly well with sun-loving aromatic plants, because its mulching properties keep the soil moist in summer and improve drainage in winter. It is available in various sizes and colours, and is softer on the eye than slate, and can be used more extensively in the garden. Pale gravel tends to look best, but you will need to choose strong shades of pink, blue and purple flowers and some equally dark foliage to add brilliance against the pale surface, as pastel flowers tend to blend into the background and disappear from view. Remember to match the size of the gravel to the scale of the plants. Diminutive alpines, for example, will need a fine scree, with perhaps the odd boulder as a visual full-stop. The drawbacks of gravel are that it is easily trodden into the house, and in urban situations gravelled areas are likely to turn into the communal cat litter tray.

Slate is another good surface for small areas; like gravel, it is best used in places that aren't walked on regularly. It can look wonderfully moody, and looks stunning with silver-leaved plants or dainty alpines, but use it in small amounts, as large expanses can look sombre and threatening. Both gravel and slate are too abrasive for sites where very young children play, as they're unfriendly on young knees.

Don't allow loose materials to drift into the soil. In summer it won't show, but when the vegetation dies back in winter, the mixture of gravel and soil at the edges simply looks messy and unfinished. To avoid this, either create an edging of wood or paving, or for a more natural look weave larger pebbles

LEFT *A pale boulder highlights the black strappy leaves of Ophiopogon planiscapus 'Nigrescens'.*

RIGHT *Square decking is given a vertical lift and gentle softening by the addition of striated stone pillars and gentle-toned saltware containers and spheres.*

among the gravel to form a firmer edge. The texture of randomly mixed pebbles is not only pleasing on the eye, but on very hot days the heat is thrown back on to the plants above, ripening the wood of tender plants (such as salvias) and encouraging tender agapanthus. Large, pale boulders also make excellent backdrops for certain plants, enhancing the dark foliage of the grass-like *Ophiopogon planiscapus* 'Nigrescens' or highlighting the bright flowers of the jaunty cyclamen.

Gravel and slate will both need refreshing every second or third year. Get your gravel delivered by the ton from a local supplier if you can, it's cheaper this way. Half-fill a wheelbarrow at a time, so it's not too heavy to push to the place where it needs to go, then fill a bucket at a time and carefully tip the gravel round the plants. Finally, rake it over very gently, using a rubber rake to pull it across. Rubber rakes can be pulled through plants without damaging stems and foliage, and one should feature in every tool collection. One ton of gravel will top-dress an area measuring about 16 square metres (172 square feet), and it's a pleasant late-winter activity. Slate is usually bought in bags and can be easily spread round plants.

BARK   Fine-textured bark is an extremely useful surface. It acts as a protective mulch, and also provides an attractive background for woodlanders and miniature bulbs, such as hellebores, snowdrops, wood anemones and pulmonarias, which will shine out against it. Bark is often a good solution in a

garden where small children play, as it is softer than gravel. Bear in mind that bark looks better in semi-shade, combined with woodland plants, than in dry, sunny sites, where it loses its rich colour and can look desiccated as well as out of place.

PAVING AND DECKING

A main path or terrace really demands a material that is strong and permanent, such as stone slabs, rather than loose materials such as gravel. If your do-it-yourself skills are as minimal as mine, you will probably need to spend money on having them laid professionally, but it will be worth every penny.

Hard surfaces tend to look better and are less slippery when they are textured rather than completely smooth, so opt for materials that provide some visual interest as well as grip. There are many imaginative ways of avoiding a rectangular mass on terraced surfaces. For example, if you leave gaps between slabs and infill them with plants, surrounded by fine gravel of a similar colour, you can break up the block effect; another option is to make a random pattern in the paving by cutting the slabs into different sizes. You can also create a staggered outline to the area, allowing you to plant low sculptural plants, such as box balls, on the outer edges, and linking the garden beyond with the paved area. Rougher, more uneven stone can be bedded into fine gravel in small areas that are not so heavily used.

Wooden decking is also a good option for a path or terrace, particularly where you want to have a variety of levels. You could use a selection of different-sized decks, or platforms, that step down to water, or down a slope. Softening these flat surfaces with curved, rounded shapes (rather than angular ones) is pleasing on the eye. Add a large round pot and perhaps two matching ceramic spheres of different sizes. Line them up with each other, the smallest sphere first, then the slightly larger sphere, and then the even larger pot. Placed like this, with the smallest leading up to the largest, they will create a perspective that leads the eye into the depths of the garden, and they can be linked visually to an interesting shape beyond. Always resist the urge to add lots of small pots: these clutter the foreground and stop the eye travelling through the garden, making the area appear smaller.

Colour themes

You may want to paint your shed or fence to make a feature; winter is a good time to experiment and to get the job done. Bear in mind that winter light changes colour perception: a sage-green seen in low winter light will fade to a muddy grey in the summer glare; if you're hesitating between two shades on a grey winter's day, opt for the darker one. One widely available colour, strong holly green, never really works in the garden. You can just about get away with it in summer, but it looks harshly stark in winter and doesn't blend with any foliage.

BELOW *Painting a shed or fence can make it a winter feature in itself. Strong colours will enhance structural forms but take care to match your choice to surrounding plantings.*

Always try to match shed and fence paint to nearby foliage; take a leaf with you when selecting paint or stain. Alternatively, go for a contrast: a pale, almost white shed will be a perfect backdrop for the May-flowering, rich violet *Allium* 'Purple Sensation', for example. Painted surfaces generally survive for two winters, at most, before they need repainting.

ABOVE *Striated pillars add
a sense of height and have been
used to add privacy to a seating
area, enclosing rustic chairs set
among dwarf conifers.*

Once you've opted for a colour, try to have echoes of similar tones in other parts of the garden, rather than using lots of colours together. You can't go wrong with shades of warm brown, copper and bronze. Add some large, salt-glazed containers, and echo the same colours in your planting – brown grasses with winter presence, such as *Carex comans* bronze, *C. testacea* and *C. flagellifera*, would all emphasise the colour theme, as well as add curving lines and swaying movement for interest.

A sense of height and enclosure

Vertical lines also become important in winter. Natural stone or irregular wooden pillars can be spaced around a seating area in a curved design, to enclose it informally while still allowing you to see the garden beyond. These pillars may measure only 1.2m (4ft) in height, but they will still give the impression of curtaining off the area and creating a feeling of enclosure. In addition, they add vertical presence, linking the garden to the sky above and leading your eye upwards.

You could use stone sarsens or driftwood, but Indian slate pillars are particularly attractive, with their striated surface colour-washed with iron-rust iridescence. The pillars' flecks of copper and blue, held in an oily pattern, could be picked up by a simple copper pot nearby, a colourful blue ceramic sphere, or a dramatic, dark-leaved phormium.

An attractive, well-placed piece of statuary, or a large container filled with a single, striking plant, can make a feature and focal point that comes into its own in winter. It's worth remembering that, in most cases, less is most definitely best, especially in a small garden.

the finishing touches

Sculptures and statuary

A well-chosen statue can really enhance a garden, and they take on extra presence in winter light. However, like homeopathy, only small amounts do the trick. I base this on visiting countless gardens where a concrete shepherdess or gushing fish meet your gaze at every turn. By the time you leave you are so disconcerted that you almost expect a troll to overpower you at the gate. Worse still, the plants in those sort of gardens are diminished rather than enhanced by the collection of weird and wonderful structures.

It is much better to limit yourself to one or two well-placed statues that have some relevance to your garden. Placing a rustic 17th-century shepherdess in a city garden wouldn't be appropriate, whereas a modern piece might well be. Once positioned, try to enhance this focal point with your planting. A dark, sombre sculpture will need a brighter background to set it off – perhaps red- and gold-stemmed willows or dogwoods (see right), or a bright evergreen holly or aucuba. Shorter bronzes, less than 1m (3ft) high, can be flattered by low-growing plants that mimic their shape, for example a swathe of swirling grasses.

Taller sculptures can be treated in two ways: they may be strong enough to stand alone, or they can be set against a background of shrubs or trees, provided they are allowed enough space to shine and as long as the plants provide a contrast to set off the sculptures, rather than camouflage. A background of winter evergreens, such as ivy, holly, yew or elaeagnus, can soften the effect of statuary

BELOW Here the warmly coloured stems of Salix alba subsp. vitellina 'Britzensis', the scarlet willow, and Cornus sanguinea 'Winter Beauty', which forms a compact bush of red, yellow and orange shoots, have been used to complement a sculpture of a young boy. The uncluttered, pebbled space around the sculpture allows the curve and stance of the boy to make full impact.

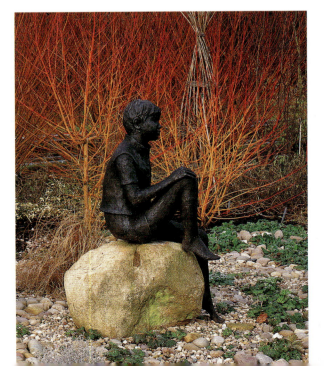

ABOVE *Swirling, tight-waisted grasses enhance these slender-necked swans without overshadowing them. The soft swirl mimics the angle of the arching necks and the brown grassy filaments flatter the bronze. The random mix of pebbles at the forefront of the swans (a mixture of beiges, rusts and browns) matches the bronze patina. The waterside location (where swans actually do roam) adds authenticity to the man-made addition.*

and tie the feature in to the rest of the garden; for the same reason, moss or lichen should be encouraged.

Rustic wooden sculptures can work in an area where there are trees, blending surrounding plants and man-made structures, but can look stark on their own. Architectural plants also make fine sculptures and add rich structure on their own, so be adventurous. Holly hedges are often trimmed to interesting shapes and conifers can add verticals.

Winter containers

You can add real highlights to the winter garden with containers filled with a mixture of fragrant, flowering or leafy winter plants. They will exude scent, provide a rich blend of leaf against a wall, or give you an early show of flowers. Once planted, these moveable feasts need little maintenance and no watering at all, and will look wonderful for two or three years – so they're easy to maintain as well as excellent value. Place your winter containers close to doorways, porches and windows where you can enjoy them, and try to add some fragrance in the form of hyacinths, sarcococcas or skimmias.

THE RIGHT POT When choosing your container for a winter arrangement, size is everything. A large pot can accommodate lots of plants, and they can protect each other from the vagaries of the weather. The ideal winter container is at least 1m (3ft) tall, and large enough to accommodate a minimum of seven plants of varying sizes and leaf textures. These plants will be sufficiently closely packed to withstand winter, while plants in small pots are likely to die in cold weather.

Winter containers need to be made from frost-hardy, solid materials. You can't get away with cheap pots. Although fine for short-term summer use, they won't withstand the freeze and thaw of an average winter. A good terracotta pot will last several lifetimes. Stone troughs, although even more expensive than terracotta, will survive for centuries, and wooden barrels will also endure for a good ten years or so. Do buy the highest-quality pot you can afford. It's much better to invest in a couple of large expensive containers to last a lifetime than in lots of smaller, cheaper pots.

Select your containers to match the style of your house and stick to a theme. If you're lucky enough to own a stylish town house, two substantial tubs in simple lines by the entrance would make an ideal addition, whether they're square Versailles planters with roundels of box, or simple terracotta pots with camellias. A country cottage is less formal, and a collection of round, salt-glazed pots, or mixed terracotta or wooden barrels, would be

BELOW *The eye is focused in this explosion of grasses and bamboos by the use of a cylindrical chimney stack and other containers with clean lines.*

RIGHT *One large container*
will make more impact than a
cluster of smaller ones. Here,
flowing ivy fronds soften the
edges and provide a delicate
contrast to the structural,
grassy leaves above.

equally acceptable. Several simple, square wooden planters, which can be
stained to soft green or grey, or left plain, are easy to accommodate close to the
house, along a terrace or path. There are also some stunning modern containers
in elliptical shapes, but experience has taught me that modern angular pots
need at least one grass-like plant to fountain upwards or tumble over the edge
to add curving line and movement. Avoid pots with narrow necks for winter
use; they become waterlogged easily, and the soil has such a small surface that
it can't dry out. Narrow-necked containers are more successful left unplanted.
The main thing to remember when choosing containers is to avoid a fussy
clutter of too many small pots in different styles; keep things simple.

SELECTING THE PLANTS   Once you have chosen your container,
consider the plants you will choose, and the relative scale of plant to pot. A
substantial square or round container measuring roughly 1m (3ft) in height and
width could accommodate plants of the same height and still look balanced,
but it's often better to limit the plant height to two-thirds of the height of the
pot. Narrow, slender containers look best when the foliage reaches only one-
third of the height of the pot, so they look elegant without being overburdened.
   The best time to plant up containers is late autumn. Go along to a large
garden centre and look at every attractive outdoor plant, mentally scoring it
out of ten as you go. Only consider plants in the peak of perfection – the
Miss Worlds of the nursery bench – and ignore any with battered leaves or

shabby branches that will spoil the show. Gather together the best they have in a trolley, choosing more foliage plants than flowering plants, because sumptuous leaves are much more important in winter than flower.

As you browse, learn to distinguish between differing colours of foliage, segregating your plants into bright greens, gold and green, cream and green, blue-greens, purples and silvers. When you've assessed what's available, decide on a foliage colour theme. Always buy more plants than you think you'll need; the leftovers can be added to the borders.

When you've gathered together a selection, try to identify a key plant. It could be a handsome grass or a stunning holly that's taken your eye. Place this in the trolley and choose the rest of the plants with that in mind, swapping and changing them about with your chosen plant at the centre. This chosen key plant needn't go bang in the centre, it can be placed off centre too. The idea is to vary the textures by choosing a mixture of strappy leaves, larger bold leaves, divided ferny foliage and tiny-leaved plants. Leave sufficient space to enable you to add a succession of miniature bulbs, single heathers and cyclamen.

BELOW *The rich purple blooms in this planting are enhanced by foliage with purple markings and tones.*

Planting a container

BEFORE YOU PLANT YOUR CONTAINER, position the pot *in situ*. By the time the soil and plants are added, the weight will be too great to move it later. If the drainage hole is small, stand the pot on feet to aid drainage. Fill the pot three-quarters full with good-quality, soil-based compost. John Innes No.2 is ideal.

Place your key plant on the ground and arrange your chosen plants around it, roughly in the shape of the container. Look at each plant individually and make sure that the plant is showing its best side (most plants have a 'back' and a 'front').

Remove the key plant from its pot by pressing firmly on the pot base and gently upending it. Check the rootball: if the roots are pot-bound, gently tease them out and straighten them. Position the key plant in the soil in a central position (it doesn't have to be completely in the middle), with the top of the rootball 1cm (½in) below the rim of the pot.

Keeping the other plants in their pots, arrange them around the key plant, angling them slightly if necessary. When you are satisfied with the arrangement, carefully remove the plants from their pots, position them in the larger container, gently firm them in and backfill with compost. Finally, remove any damaged leaf tips and untangle the plants by running your fingers gently through the foliage, rather like a hairdresser. Water the container thoroughly after planting.

Feed during summer, using a nitrogen-rich plant food every month. This will keep the evergreen leaves glossy for next winter.

Plants for containers

Listed below are plants that work well in winter containers:

EVERGREEN SHRUBS

Aucuba japonica – high-gloss plant with large green leaves liberally speckled with bright gold.

Hebe 'Emerald Gem' (syn. 'Green Globe') – invaluable, tight bun-shaped mound of bright green leaves.

Ilex aquifolium 'Ferox Argentea' (hedgehog holly) – compact, slow-growing, mound-forming male holly with prickles all over the leaf.

Ilex aquifolium 'Green Pillar' – upright, slender female with dark green leaves and red berries.

Ilex aquifolium 'Myrtifolia' – dense, neat male holly with purple shoots and small, elliptical, dark green leaves edged in spines.

Osmanthus heterophyllus 'Goshiki' – holly-like leaves mottled in green and yellow.

Osmanthus heterophyllus 'Gulftide' – a slow-growing holly look-alike with twisted, dark green leaves and fragrant white flowers.

Sarcococca confusa – scented evergreen with shiny pointed leaves and highly scented, ivory-white bundles of stamens.

Skimmia x *confusa* 'Kew Green' – large, conical heads of green buds.

Skimmia japonica subsp. *reevesiana* – crimson-red fruits.

Skimmia japonica 'Rubella' – clusters of wine-red buds.

Viburnum tinus – clusters of pale pink or white flowers.

STEMS AND SKELETONS

Cornus alba 'Kesselringii' – dogwood with purple-black stems.

Cornus alba 'Sibirica' (syn 'Weston-birt') – the brightest red dogwood.

Cornus sanguinea 'Winter Beauty' – twiggy orange and red stems.

Cornus sericea 'Flaviramea' – straight, substantial, olive-green stems.

Corylus avellana 'Contorta' – corkscrew stems and catkins.

LEAFY PERENNIALS

Bergenia 'Bressingham Ruby' – large, glossy leaves.

Helleborus foetidus 'Wester Flisk Group' – green flowers and divided, matt foliage touched with red.

Heuchera 'Purple Petticoats' – frilly, dusky-purple leaves.

Polypodium vulgare – the most rugged of the evergreen ferns.

Vinca minor 'Atropurpurea' (lesser periwinkle) – trailing plant with plum-purple flowers.

GRASS-LIKE FOLIAGE

Acorus gramineus 'Ogon' – erect fountain of green and gold.

Carex morrowii 'Variegata' – solid olive-green leaves margined cream.

Carex testacea – tightly-waisted swirl of fine, olive-green to brown leaves with tints of orange.

Luzula sylvatica 'Aurea' – soft, butter-yellow rosette.

Ophiopogon planiscapus 'Nigrescens' – low-growing black rosette.

Stunning combinations

BRIGHT AND CHEERY – Green- and gold-variegated leaves, such as box, holly or leafy euonymus, combine well with plain green foliage and yellow flowers (early **crocus, daffodils, primroses, aconites, celandines**) or blue flowers (**crocus, scillas, hyacinths, primulas**, *Anemone blanda*) to create a cheerful mixture.

DRAMATIC MIX – Bright green leaves with added touches of warm red, for

example a mini cyclamen or a red-berried *Gaultheria procumbens*, will add vitality. For further drama, add the black grass-like *Ophiopogon planiscapus* 'Nigrescens'. This shines when used with deep red, and is one of the most useful winter container plants.

DARK AND LIGHT CONTRASTS – All dramatic, dark-leaved plants, for example dark purple heucheras and bergenias, can be combined with silver hebes (*Hebe pimeleoides* 'Quicksilver') and paler grasses (*Carex comans* 'Frosted Curls', *Stipa tenuissima*, *Festuca glauca* 'Blauglut' or 'Blaufuchs') to great effect.

REDS AND PINKS – The cooler wine-red foliage of *Heuchera* 'Palace Purple Select', *Phormium* 'Bronze Baby' or 'Sundowner' can be used with dark green leaves and pale pink flowers, such as **hellebores, heathers** (*Erica* 'Winter Beauty') and pink primroses (*Primula* 'Guinevere', 'Barbara Midwinter').

COOL HARMONIES – Green and cream creates a calm, peaceful blend; *Sarcococca confusa* mixed with *Skimmia* 'Kew Green', with a background of mottled **aucubas**, takes some beating.

GOOD WITH GRASSES – Brown grasses, such as *Carex*, look stunning surrounded by blue *Anemone blanda* by the time spring arrives.

FRAGRANT MIX – For a scented container, combine forced blue hyacinths with contrasting pale yellow primroses, *Crocus chrysanthus* 'Cream Beauty' and *Narcissus* 'February Gold'.

jewels
against
bare
earth

6

For the first half of winter, most of our visual pleasure is derived from leafy evergreens, the tracery and texture provided by deciduous woody plants, or the decaying remnants of summer in the form of seedheads, hips, berries and haws. But as the days lengthen, fresh buds begin to unfurl, revealing soft, pristine petals, causing a great stirring in the gardener's soul.

fresh flowers unfurl

The earliest flowers tend to appear at ground level. The first to brave the winter may be a single snowdrop piercing the soil with its pointed, green-tipped blade, or a hunched-up winter aconite, straightening its short neck to show off its butter-yellow globe while pushing back those feathery tendrils of leaf. The jaunty cyclamen, with its swept-back petals and wind-tunnel profile, may stand defiant, or a siren crocus may open just wide enough to lure a sleepy bee into its warm, protective chalice. Whichever hero grabs the honour of being first, gardeners instantly sense that the pendulum has begun to move the other way, and that a new and exciting gardening year is about to begin.

LEFT *The jaunty Cyclamen* coum *pushes bravely upwards.*

RIGHT *Winter aconites (Eranthis hyemalis) and single snowdrops (Galanthus nivalis) battle it out to win the title of first flower of the year.*

PREVIOUS PAGES *Delicate wood anemones, the pink-backed Anemone nemorosa 'Westwell Park' and the pale A. x lipsiensis 'Pallida' light up the soil.*

The warm-up act

Although most fresh flowers start appearing from midwinter onwards, there are a few plants that are capable of unfurling fresh buds from late autumn. These early flowers often bloom from early winter, and are always worth growing. I rely on three in particular – the winter jasmine (*Jasminium nudiflorum*, see page 140), *Iris unguicularis*, and a tiny daffodil (*Narcissus* 'Cedric Morris').

Iris unguicularis, an Algerian species iris, likes a hot, dry bake at the base of a sunny wall, where it will form a wide clump of thin leaves measuring up to 60cm (2ft). It will unfurl the odd flower in late autumn, its petals pushing open a slender, translucent bud that seems to appear from nowhere, then it will keep sending out stray flowers throughout winter, finishing with a full flourish in early spring. I once estimated that one clump measuring 60cm (2ft) wide had produced about 60 flowers over winter, possibly more. Pick a flower

As the second half of winter unfolds, several low-growing plants work their jewel-like charm against the dark tapestry of bare earth. At any other time of year, these diminutive plants would so easily be lost, but now – when most flowers are still cowering below the surface – they push bravely upwards, making an impact on the garden far out of proportion to their size.

mid to late winter gems

These early jewels look best planted in groups, preferably among larger spring-flowering perennials, trees and shrubs. They will also look much better concentrated in one place than peppered thinly throughout the garden. If you're starting from scratch, look for a sheltered site, where frost doesn't linger for long, and set about making a splash.

Most early flowers benefit from a protective canopy provided by deciduous trees or shrubs. This allows light and warmth to strike the ground between early autumn and early spring, when the leaves are absent and the exposure to light prompts early-flowering plants into growth. In summer, the leafy canopy expands, keeping the area cool and shaded while the woodlanders lie dormant. Another benefit of planting alongside trees and shrubs is that the close presence of woody plant roots removes moisture from the soil, reducing the chance of frost and keeping the ground warm and friable, even in winter. You'll notice this when digging towards a tree or shrub – wet, sticky soil quite suddenly gives way to well-drained loam. If the trees and shrubs close by are spring-flowering, such as early viburnums or spicy witch hazel (*Hamamelis*), so much the better, as the visual impact will be greater.

You can use a mixture of earlier-flowering diminutives under your canopy, including snow-drops and cyclamen, as well as later-flowering plants such as wood anemones, small miniature daffodils, hepaticas and certain enduring corydalis. These can all be woven through larger, more

BELOW *The drier areas under tall trees are perfect for early spring-flowering* Cyclamen coum.

substantial perennials, principally hellebores and pulmonarias, to create an area that peaks in the second half of winter.

Loftier background plants

Hellebores and pulmonarias will provide an excellent background for diminutive additions, because their compact habit doesn't swamp the smaller plants. As with any plants you are using in large numbers, hellebores and pulmonarias look better planted in drifts, threading through the garden in a wavy ribbon of three, five, seven or nine plants, rather than grouped together in large clumps.

CHOICE HELLEBORES The late British gardening writer Christopher Lloyd once referred to hellebore enthusiasts as 'hell -i -bores', and I must confess to being one of those. Hellebores are such wonderful garden plants, and they are second to none in giving real winter value. Their flowers, which consist of tough bracts rather than soft petals, open in midwinter or late winter but continue to keep a presence until late spring, and their glossy foliage is on show for ten months of the year.

In midwinter, every early flower show and garden centre bench will present you with hybrid hellebores. These are bred from a mix of several species and they should be labelled *Helleborus* x *hybridus*, although they may possibly still be sold under their former name of Oriental hellebore (*H.* x *orientalis*). Their common name is the Lenten rose, so named because of their habit of flowering during Lent, a movable period between Christmas and Easter. These hybrid hellebores have several advantages over the single species – they are hardier, more vigorous, and there is a great diversity of flower colour and shape owing to the mix of species, giving you maximum choice.

The colours of *Helleborus* x *hybridus* vary enormously, and include pure white, pale yellow, apricot, apple-blossom pink, clear-red, plum, blue-black and wine. The petals can be a single colour, spotted, or streaked. Dark hellebores are lovely close up, but they tend to merge into the soil, so they need the contrast of light-coloured background plants to prevent them from fading into obscurity. You could set sombre-coloured hellebores against a pale silver-birch trunk or low-growing evergreen, such as *Daphne laureola,* for example. Alternatively, position them close to a sweep of early daffodils or snowdrops, or the pale sheath of fine leaves provided by *Miscanthus sinensis* 'Morning Light'. Paler hellebores generally make more of an impact on the eye be new growth shooting from the base. Most hellebores are sold in deep pots, like the ones often used for roses. If your hellebore's roots are woven round, forming a circular mass, tear off the roots and deliberately damage them by pulling them downwards sharply. This will help the plant to make new roots, allowing it to penetrate your soil.

The foliage of all hellebores can suffer from a fungal black spot disease called *Coniothyrium hellebori*, which shows itself by forming papery, dark blotches on the leaf. The easiest way to avoid this disease is to buy a really healthy plant in the first place, but you should also remove every leaf in late autumn or early winter (the exception is *Helleborus* x *ericsmithii*, which should be left intact). If fungal black spot begins to get a grip, remove affected leaves as soon as you spot a mark, however small, and dispose of them (never add diseased leaves to a compost heap). As a preventive measure, you can also discourage the disease by applying a fine bark or compost mulch round each hellebore in late summer. This stops the spores from being washed back up from soil to leaf by rain splash. Take care not to cover the crown with mulch, as it may cause rot.

BELOW *The brick-red flowers of Pulmonaria rubra 'Barfield Ruby' emerge early, but this green-leaved pulmonaria needs space – it's a spreader.*

PROMISCUOUS PULMONARIAS My other late winter to spring staple is the pulmonaria or lungwort, so named because their often spotted leaves are thought to resemble diseased lungs. Some are grown primarily for their foliage, but there are others that produce attractive flowers.

Pulmonarias produce clusters of nectar-rich blooms that unfold in early spring, giving weeks of flower, and the bees adore them. Some have the forget-me-not habit of changing colour after pollination: the pink flowers turn blue, and this two-tone, motley look has given rise to one of the common names, soldiers and sailors, harking back to the days when soldiers wore red and sailors blue.

The earliest variety to flower in my garden is always the plain-leaved, unspotted *Pulmonaria rubra*. This produces warm, tomato-red flowers and forms a large, open clump. It is best accommodated in larger woodland gardens and doesn't do well in smaller spaces. However, there is a more compact, variegated form called var. *albocorollata* 'David Ward' (named after the propagator who worked at Beth Chatto's nursery, where it first arose). Although lovely, this form needs a shady, sheltered site to thrive, as well as regular division.

When bumble bees visit pulmonarias, these promiscuous plants reproduce freely and the resulting seedlings are variable. This has led to

at least 200 named pulmonarias, although inevitably many are similar. A good, vigorous variety is *Pulmonaria* Opal ('Ocupol'), with attractive pale, almost grey flowers. The much-heralded *P.* 'Sissinghurst White' is indeed charmingly pretty, but it lacks vigour and makes a gappy plant. Of those with distinctive spotted or silvered foliage and blue flowers, *P.* 'Trevi Fountain', *P.* 'Lewis Palmer' and *P. longifolia* 'Ankum' are all reliably good. 'Trevi Fountain' is a short, free-flowering pulmonaria topped with tightish clusters of small cobalt-blue flowers; 'Lewis Palmer' has dense heads of dark blue flowers; and 'Ankum' is a later-flowering, dark blue variety with long, silvered leaves.

The deepest, darkest blues usually have *Pulmonaria angustifolia* blood. They tend to be later-flowering, with unspotted leaves. The intense blue *P.* 'Blue Ensign' is the most desirable hybrid form. However, they need moister, richer soil than most other pulmonarias, and I've struggled with them in my dry, stony garden. One I've done better with is the violet-red, plain-leaved *P. mollis*.

Real reds are few and far between. *Pulmonaria saccharata* 'Leopard' has upright stems bearing small clusters of brick-red flowers and is the best warm red. The blooms of *P.* 'Mary Mottram' start red and then turn to violet. *P.* 'Victorian Brooch' is a neat magenta-coral, and *P. saccharata* 'Mrs Moon' a purple-red. *P.* 'Raspberry Splash' produces small pink-red flowers and heavily spotted leaves.

There are two rather dainty pulmonarias with tiny leaves and flowers, one in baby pink (*P.* 'Mrs Kittle') and the other in baby blue (*P.* 'Roy Davidson'). Both are ideal plants for smaller gardens but need regular division to thrive.

Pulmonarias' penchant for interbreeding can be a mixed blessing. Their seedlings are adept at invading a choice hellebore or smothering a clump of prized snowdrops. To prevent pulmonarias from self-seeding, I tend to dead-head in late spring, when most of the flowers are over (I still get seedlings, but not as many). At the same time, I also cut off all the leaves. This scalping is followed by a welcome bucket of warm water containing a nitrogen-rich feed intended to stimulate fresh summer leaves. You could either buy a soluble, nitrogen-rich fertiliser, or you could make your own liquid feed. To do this, put comfrey leaves or nettle foliage in a bucket, allow the leaves to decompose, dilute the resulting liquid with some warm water, and pour over the plants.

Early-flowering diminutives

It is the earliest flowers of all that stir the already restless gardener's soul, and the snowdrop is often the first to appear *en masse*. Keen gardeners will travel miles to enjoy a sweep of the common snowdrop (*Galanthus nivalis*), however bleak the weather. And if tulipomania gripped Dutch gardeners in the 17th century, arousing avarice and greed, galanthophilia has replaced it in the present day. Indeed, I have seen many a rugged male pluck a small mirror from his jacket pocket and place it underneath a flower in order to fully admire the inner markings, or they get down on bended knee as if in homage. The following flowers could be with you by midwinter if the weather is sufficiently mild.

SNOWDROPS AND SNOWFLAKES The mania for snowdrops has led to hundreds of named forms, and this can sometimes be bewildering, particularly as some of the differences are barely perceptible. To me, a good garden snowdrop has to be vigorous (not 'miffy') and distinctive in some way. The ones described here are all readily available, easy to grow, and offer something special for the garden. Their exquisite white flowers are perfect for lighting up the ground under trees and shrubs in winter.

If this is your first attempt at growing snow-drops, start off with the common *Galanthus nivalis*, the ones you often see in churchyards, as these are the most reliable and least expensive of all snowdrops. There is a single form (known simply as *G. nivalis*) and a double form (labelled *G. nivalis* 'Flore Pleno'). You can buy common snowdrops 'in the green', in their hundreds, in early spring. Simply separate the clumps and plant them in a semi-shaded place, preferably in groups of three. When the clump looks full (this usually takes about three years), separate the plants, carefully lifting them just as the flowers fade, and then

BELOW *Tall Greatorex doubles do well in the garden. The relatively shallow blooms nod atop tall, strong stems.*

replant them somewhere else in the garden. Once you have succeeded with the easiest snowdrop of all, progress to the more expensive specialist varieties.

The tall, elegant single snowdrop *Galanthus* 'Atkinsii' has narrow white outer petals that open widely, reminding me of an open tripod set at 45 degrees. This is early, upright and slender, and is generally one of the first to finish flowering, so place it somewhere towards the back, where the dying foliage won't mar later-flowering plants. Another fine, tall, single snowdrop is 'Magnet'. Each single snowdrop bloom is suspended from a fine arc of long, wiry stem. It's often possible to spot 'Magnet' just by the way the graceful, curved stems and flowers tremble and flutter in the slightest breeze.

RIGHT *A small vase of my own named snowdrops show the many lovely variations.*

The greyer-leaved *Galanthus elwesii* is a robust, variable single snowdrop from Turkey, and there are many handsome named forms. It tends to be relatively upright, because the leaves are held together tightly by a papery sheath at ground level. If you were to cut through the leafy base, the leaves would be arranged in rings, rather like a leek. The flowers are held on stiff stems at a shy, downward-facing angle. They usually have two heavy mid-green markings, an upper bar and a lower inverted 'V', and are topped with dark green oval ovaries. Each bulb is large, almost the size of a miniature daffodil (maddeningly, sometimes very big bulbs can produce insignificant, tiny flowers). All greyer-leaved snowdrops are happiest in a more open position at the front of a woodland area.

Galanthus woronowii is a low-growing snowdrop, which is being imported from Georgia in large numbers. It has relatively wide, emerald-green leaves and small, globular, bright white single flowers. It keeps its shiny, green leaves well and they are a wonderful foil for slightly later-flowering plants. You may also be able to find *G. plicatus*, another snowdrop with wide green leaves, often faintly vertically striped in lighter grey-green. If you look at the reverse side of the leaves, at the base where they emerge from the bulb, you will see that the outer edges are pleated backwards, giving rise to the species name, *plicatus*, meaning pleated. This is a vigorous snowdrop that is good in shade and strong enough to push though ground-cover planting, such as ivy or vinca, to display its white single flowers. The outer petals often have a seer-sucker texture, and the inners usually have one green mark. I've also seen this snowdrop growing in grass in the wild. 'Wendy's Gold', with yellow markings, was originally found growing in low grass among a large colony on the top of Wandlebury Ring, near Cambridge. Many snowdrops with yellow markings are shy to increase, but 'Wendy's Gold' is an exception.

Galanthus 'S. Arnott' is a giant single snowdrop that can reach up to 25cm (10in) on good soil. The pendant, pearl-drop flowers open widely and smell of honey, and many a gardener has been seduced by its beauty, size and sweet fragrance. It has a very deep green, heart-shaped mark on the lowest edge of the inner petals and elegant lines. A large colony of 'S. Arnott' once grew near Stroud and the bulbs were lifted and sold by The Giant Snowdrop Company in the years following World War II. 'S. Arnott' caught the public imagination and even made the front pages of the newspaper. It rekindled interest in snowdrops, inspiring a fresh band of galanthophiles (as snowdrop-lovers have come to be known) in the 1960s.

It's a good idea to have some double-flowered snowdrops as well as elegant singles, but choose carefully as some can be ragged and untidy once you lift the flowers upwards and gaze into their middles. Heyrick Greatorex, an amateur breeder from Brundell, Norfolk, set about breeding a whole series of fine, tall, strong-growing doubles from the 1930s until his death in 1954. Most of his cultivars have Shakespearian or Classical names. There is *Galanthus* 'Jacquenetta', 'Dionysus', 'Titania', 'Cordelia', 'Desdemona', 'Ophelia' and 'Hippolyta'. Greatorex doubles are excellent in the garden setting. You can identify them by their stance – a tall, strong stem with a small, full flower perched on top. The shallowness of the flower in comparison to the length of the stem is also a Greatorex double trademark. On examination, each flower has a shallow tutu of tight inners, surrounded by shortish, outer petals. The markings are dark holly green, and these similar Greatorex varieties are difficult to tell apart.

The low-growing apricot and white flowers of the capricious *G. nivalis* f. *pleniflorus* 'Lady Elphinstone' can (and do) revert to plain green. But when she's behaving well, she's a lovely addition, with her egg-yolk markings. You might also be able to find *G.* 'Lady Beatrix Stanley', an early snowdrop with distinctive grey-green leaves and wide flowers, likened to a molar tooth in shape, and held on short stems.

There are also lots of misshapen, freakish snowdrops, including the fanged *Galanthus* 'Walrus' and the 'Green Horror', also known as 'Boyd's Double'. This love of the aberrant can be traced back to the greatest galanthophile of all, Edward Augustus Bowles (1865–1954). Bowles housed a great number of odd and weird plants in his 'lunatic asylum', which can still be seen today in his Myddleton House garden, at Bull's Cross, near Enfield in Middlesex. But the best of the misshapen snowdrops found in recent times is the cheeky *G. nivalis* f. *pleniflorus* 'Blewbury Tart'. This tight double is dark green and white, and

LEFT *Galanthus* 'Cordelia' *is one of the strong-growing, tall Greatorex doubles that is well worth planting.*

ABOVE *The cheeky Galanthus nivalis f. pleniflorus 'Blewbury Tart' has green upward-facing flowers and bulks up well.*

each frilled flower looks upward at a cock-eyed angle. It's good at bulking up, flowers very well and is low-growing. It was discovered in 1975 by English nurseryman Alan Street, who grew up in Blewbury, Oxfordshire. I'm sure that Edward Bowles would have thoroughly approved of this coquettish little flower.

If you're thinking of growing snowdrops, don't forget to include their close relation, the spring-flowering snowflake, *Leucojum vernum*, which often flowers with the snowdrop. It is slightly larger than a snowdrop and usually bears two crinoline- or bell-shaped flowers. Each of the six white petals is tipped in green. Like all leucojums, it is happiest in moist soil. Divide the clumps when necessary, just as you do with snowdrops. There is also a leucojum with yellow tips on the petals, *L. vernum* var. *carpathicum*, although I have not found this as strong or enduring as the green-tipped species.

JAUNTY, SWEPT-BACK CYCLAMEN

Another dainty plant that flowers in winter is *Cyclamen coum*, with its rounded leaves, sometimes marked with silver patterns, and compact flowers, in white or pink with magenta markings around the nose. The cyclamen prefers a more open position than the snowdrop, being a native of Greece, Italy and the Balearics, as well as other warm regions. A summer bake is very much appreciated by all cyclamen, and not all the species are fully hardy. Some demand the added protection of a bulb frame or alpine house in winter.

The best way to introduce early cyclamen into your garden is to buy pot-grown *Cyclamen coum* in winter and plant them out. Again, just as with snowdrops, there are many named forms and subspecies, but when trying anything for the first time, always opt for a standard form. You will only need five potfuls of cyclamen to begin with, because they all set seed. The resulting curious seedpods are held on coiled, corkscrew-like stems, rather like a miniature dog whelk's purse washed up on a beach. These round cyclamen purses open in summer, and the seeds are easy to collect; you can actually hear them rattling when they're ripe. Seeds should be sown straight away. You can either sprinkle them straight onto the ground by hand, or you can sow them in a greenhouse or cold frame: place the seeds on the surface in a pot of well-drained compost, then cover them with a layer of fine grit. If you forget to collect any seeds, don't worry; the ants will disperse them for you – you'll be amazed at where they come up.

A. ranunculoides called *A.* x *lipsiensis* 'Pallida'. This bulks up very slowly, but do seek it out – its pale yellow flowers are as radiant as moonlight on a still night.

In the garden setting, wood anemones need moist, humus-rich, friable soil. If you can, add your own leaf mould, or allow leaves to decompose above them.

WOODLAND BUTTERCUPS The lesser celandine (*Ranunculus ficaria*), a woodland buttercup, was the favourite flower of the romantic English poet William Wordsworth (1770–1850). He even asked for the flower to be carved on his tombstone, but the stonemason gave him the greater celandine, *Chelidonium majus,* in error. Wordsworth wrote:

> *There is a flower, the lesser celandine*
> *That shrinks, like many more, from cold and rain*
> *And, the first moment that the sun may shine*
> *Bright as the sun himself, 'tis out again.*

Although much loved by Wordsworth, many gardeners have mixed feelings about lesser celandines. While they certainly have beautiful, jaunty, lacquered yellow flowers and small, neat leaves, their tubers produce masses of tiny offsets that can be extremely invasive and difficult to remove. And yet some single celandines can be so alluring – take *Ranunculus ficaria* 'Brazen Hussy', with her almost black leaves and vivid single yellow flowers, or 'Coppernob', in a soft orange with veined leaves. Or perhaps the creamy-white 'Randall's White' or the very veiny-leaved white 'Brambling'. When planting celandines, bear in mind their invasive quality, and site them where they are allowed to spread, for example in a large area of woodland garden.

Double celandines are more reluctant to set seed, and if you add these to the woodland garden and leave them undisturbed, the nuisance factor of countless seedlings should be greatly reduced. Well-behaved doubles include the yellow *Ranunculus ficaria* 'Collarette', or the wonderfully named 'Yaffle', a concoction of woodpecker-green and cream flowers. Then there's 'Double Mud', a frilled cream, and 'Double Bronze', a dark-edged yellow.

OTHER WOODLANDERS Hepaticas, or liverworts, are closely related to the wood anemone (*Anemone nemorosa*) and they have three- or five-lobed leaves and similar flowers in white, blue or pink. The most commonly grown is *Hepatica nobilis*, and although this is often thought of as an alpine plant I have grown them on the edges of my woodland garden with great success. The white-flowered forms are excellent in the woodland garden,

BELOW *The dark leaves of this lesser celandine* Ranunculus ficaria *'Brazen Hussy' set off the bright yellow flowers.*

ABOVE Hepatica nobilis *is a close relative of wood anemones and there are whites, good blues and pink forms.*

because they stand out so well, and the blues and pinks have an intensity of colour lacking in the wood anemones. All have dark foliage and self-seed, sometimes a little too well. The Japanese have developed some amazing forms in every flower type and colour, but these make poor garden plants, and are really best grown as specimens in pots. I have also grown a larger hepatica, with sky-blue flowers and larger, rounder, greener leaves called H. x *media* 'Harvington Beauty'. This keeps its leaves through winter and then sends up clear-blue flowers in early spring.

You could also add the tiny clump-former *Hacquetia epipactis* to a shady place. Its small centre of tiny flowers is surrounded by a leafy ring of large green bracts, just like the ray florets on a daisy. The plain species has greenish-yellow bracts. 'Thor' is a new variety, with cream margins set round these bracts. Both are crisply neat in form and show up well against dark soil.

Another late woodlander, the dog's tooth violet, or erythronium, makes its mark in late winter with its attractive marbled foliage. The leaves are followed in early to mid-spring by pendant, lily-like flowers which come in a variety of colours from the ivory 'White Beauty', to the yellow 'Pagoda' to 'Pink Perfection'. When growing in the wild, mainly in North America, the bulb springs to life when the snow-melt arrives, so their main priority is to ensure that they do not dry out. However, they also dislike being waterlogged and standing in cold, wet conditions. Leaf mould and garden compost in abundance will help to improve the soil condition.

Gardeners tend to be seduced by the pale cornflower-blue corydalis from China, usually *Corydalis flexuosa*, which flowers in early summer, but these are not enduring garden plants. However, the tuberous early-flowering *C. solida*, with its ferny divided leaves, is considerably longer-lasting. While some forms produce racemes of washed-out blue or grey-pink flowers, there are some first-rate named varieties in stronger colours. *C. solida* subsp. *solida* 'George

Baker' is a rich red, 'Snowlark' is a creamy white, 'Highland Mist' is a smoky grey-pink, and 'Beth Evans' is a heather pink. These thrive in an open position (perhaps close to hardy geraniums, which only send out their leaves after the tiny corydalis have finished), or they could be grown in troughs or in a rock garden.

PRIMROSES AND POLYANTHUS   Rather romantically, the name primrose comes from *prima rosa*, meaning the first rose in Latin, a reference to their beautiful early flowers. Although I would discourage you from growing our native primrose, *Primula vulgaris*, on the grounds that it is both overly common as well as invasive once the leaves expand in summer, I would advise you to use some named varieties.

The earliest primrose for me is always the bright pink *Primula* 'Barbara Midwinter'; unfortunately, it can be hard to find. 'Lady Greer' is a refined, pale yellow polyanthus with longer leaves, and is useful because it forms a tight clump. The seed-raised Barnhaven primroses come in deep reds, strong blues, tobacco-browns and many other colours. They are dazzling, and do well in the

ABOVE *'White Beauty' is one of the best erythroniums. All have good, often marbled, foliage and downward-facing flowers of great charm; in fertile, humus-rich soil they bulk up well.*

garden, and are available as young plants or seeds. Don't be tempted by the giant-flowered bedders, with large, brash flowers on short, squat stems. While they are fine for park bedding, woodlanders are subtle and subdued.

The Wanda Group, single hybrids bred from *Primula juliae*, have larger flowers that are earlier than typical primroses, in deep colours, attractively centred in yellow. The purple-red *P*. 'Wanda' and its offspring form low mounds and are long-lived, hardy plants. 'Guinevere' is a pretty pink with beetroot-red leaves, and 'Schneekissen' (translated as 'Snow Cushion') is a low-growing small white.

Double primroses with frilled flowers have always been prized, and many make enduring garden plants. *Primula vulgaris* 'Lilacina Plena' (syn. 'Quaker's Bonnet'), possibly a 17th-century variety, is a loose double in soft lilac. 'Lilian Harvey' is a strong pink, 'Miss Indigo' is a silver-edged navy-blue, and 'Marie Crousse' a pink-purple double. Micropropagation has bulked these doubles up enormously, making them more readily available. However, many of the plants you see for sale have come from a greenhouse and are grown in peaty compost, so they need to be nurtured when young.

In some varieties, one primrose flower seems to grow inside another. These were named 'hose-in-hose' by the Elizabethans, who adopted the fashion of wearing short doublets and two pairs of hose – one inside the other – to keep themselves warm in winter. There are hose-in-hose forms of 'Wanda' and our common primrose, *Primula vulgaris*. If the flower was ringed in a ruff of leaf it was named 'Jack in the Pulpit' or 'Jack in the Green', and there are still various forms bearing these names today. 'Dawn Ansell' is a superb modern white with a green ruff.

All winter- to spring-flowering primroses benefit from regular division after flowering, but only when the clumps begin to look too compacted and full of stem. Divide the clumps and replant them out in moist, cool shade, or pot them up into gritty compost. Dividing them will help to deter vine weevil infestation too. Primroses hate drying out and prefer a cool-summer root run. For this reason, they are difficult to keep in a pot for longer than a season.

VIOLETS Violets can also be invasive, owing to their habit of self-seeding and spreading by stolons, so I've always tended to place them close to primroses but away from diminutive snowdrops and wood anemones. They often flower from late winter onwards, when few pollinators are about. As an insurance policy, some violets also produce

BELOW *The striking double flowers of Primula 'Miss Indigo' are an inky-blue finely edged in silver-white.*

summer flowers that don't open but can still produce viable seeds without a pollinator. Good early-flowering garden forms include the scented pink *Viola* 'Norah Church', the deep purple 'The Czar', the purple-blue 'Baroness De Rothschild' and the white 'Mrs R. Barton'.

MINIATURE DAFFODILS There are many miniature daffodils, or narcissi, that appear early enough to be included in this winter book. Miniature varieties work well early in the year: they are less prone to being

blown about by the weather, and their scale (under 5cm/2in in diameter) matches that of other diminutive early plants. To get early flowers, choose an open, warm position that gets afternoon sun.

Miniatures have all been bred from early Spanish species, and many of the best were creations of Alec Gray (1895–1986), a Cornish grower of daffodils for the cut-flower trade. He tried to cross classic cut-flower varieties with early Spanish species in the hopes of breeding tall, early daffodils that would earn him more money at the flower market. Instead, he produced the first miniatures, including the fabulous *Narcissus* 'Tête-à-tête', registered in 1949 and named for the fact that it sometimes bears two golden yellow, trumpeted flowers per stem. He also bred the multi-headed, clear yellow 'Jumblie', which has backward-sweeping petals. Other good early miniatures include the golden yellow 'February Gold', the long-trumpeted golden yellow 'Peeping Tom', and the primrose-yellow 'Quince'.

Narcissus 'Rijnveld's Early Sensation' is the earliest of the taller daffodils (growing about 38cm/15in high), and is well worth planting, although it must be divided regularly. 'Jetfire' is just over a miniature in height, at 22–30cm (9–12in) high, but this yellow daffodil develops a bright orange trumpet, the nearest there is to a red trumpet of all the shorter daffodils, making it a cheering sight.

Yellow daffodils generally flower before the paler creams and whites. If you want to line a drive with daffodils, or plant them under trees, it is a good idea to mix a yellow variety with white to give a longer season of flower. The classic creamy-white variety for mass planting is *Narcissus* 'Mount Hood', and this could be combined with the strong yellow 'Carlton'.

Winter-flowering sun-worshippers

Although many early-flowering plants like being overshadowed with a canopy of leaf, there are those that embrace the sun. Winter aconites (*Eranthis hyemalis*), spring-flowering crocuses, early dwarf irises (*Iris reticulata* and *I. histrioides*) and *Anemone blanda* all prefer dry, warm conditions.

LEFT *This old variety, Narcissus Tête-à-Tête, certainly provides value, as it can produce two flowers per stem when truly happy.*

SUN-BAKED CROCUSES Crocuses hail from hot, dry, rocky sites in Turkey, Greece and North Africa. They are also found in the high mountainous regions of Europe, including Austria and Italy. Although there are over 80 species worldwide, as well as many subspecies, gardeners tend to rely on just three kinds of crocus. All prefer open, well-drained sites. They flower as early as midwinter if it is sufficiently mild, or may not flower until early spring if temperatures are lower.

Most of the crocuses with large, goblet-shaped flowers in purple, part-purple or pure-white are Dutch selections bred from *Crocus vernus*, the species found in the European Alps. These giants have the strength to push through dense turf, which makes them useful in bulb lawns among robust early daffodils such as *Narcissus* 'Jetfire'. Good forms of Dutch crocus include the purple-striped *C. vernus* 'Pickwick', the deep silver-purple 'Remembrance' and the pale blue 'Queen of the Blues'. Dutch crocuses bulk up quickly, and many of the varieties that were bred in the first half of the 20th century are still going strong. They can persist in a garden for decades, forming larger and larger clumps.

Sunny oranges and creams are usually bred from *Crocus chrysanthus*, a more diminutive species from the Balkans and Turkey. These are early to flower and have smaller, cup-shaped flowers. *C. chrysanthus* 'Cream Beauty' (one of my personal favourites) is a soft creamy yellow. 'Blue Pearl' is pale blue with a yellow throat, and 'Ladykiller' is a white crocus heavily striped in purple on the outer petals, although you can only see the purple stripes when the

BOTTOM *Early-flowering Crocus chrysanthus 'Cream Beauty' will produce its deliciously buttery blooms in a well-drained, sunny site.*

the
flowering
canopy

7

As winter progresses, twiggy branches that look all but dead will show a sudden pinprick of colour at the very tip of each bud before unfurling their petals. Amazingly, these midwinter flowers are often very fragrant. If the temperature rises to a clement 12°C (54°F) or above, the strength of fragrance intensifies further, and the flowers become a potent lure for an early pollinator.

flowers on bare branches

These bare-branch flowers are always subtle in colour and delicate in form. If they were large and showy, winter weather would batter and tear them. Their delicate scale matches the diminutive flowers studding the bare earth in both size and shade: there's a soft palette of pale pink, creamy white, lemon yellow and soft greens.

The first to flower

The winter jasmine, although common, is a superb winter shrub. In mild years, its acid-yellow flowers break out all along the twiggy branches from late autumn until early spring. If you want really early flowers, grow it in full sun. Although tolerant of shade, the flowers appear much later in shady sites. Winter jasmine is ideal up against the side of the house or framing a doorway. You can also fashion it into a low hedge, or sculpt it into a walk-through arch. Pruning is simple: just take the shears and trim the growth back after flowering. The twiggy branches of winter jasmine can be used in arrangements, and their yellow flowers contrast particularly well with the blue winter iris, *Iris unguicularis*.

The ribboned witch hazel

Among the first twigs of flower to brave midwinter are those of the witch hazel. Their branching, shrubby framework supports flowers in shades of pale lemon, but there are also brash golds, citrus-oranges, spice-browns and warm reds as well. These flowers, which often have a warm, oriental fragrance, consist of narrow, ribboned petals

BELOW *Winter jasmine (Jasminum nudiflorum) produces olive-green twigs and bright yellow, starry flowers. Every garden should have at least one.*

PREVIOUS PAGES *The delicate blooms of Hamamelis mollis (witch hazel) will glow against a clear winter sky.*

RIGHT *Witch hazel flowers are spidery collections of ribbon-like petals held in dark calices. They are a delight to look at, and can be spicily scented too.*

curving outwards from a central collection of dark calices – like spiders with crêpe-paper legs, they unfurl and dangle. However cold the weather, these resilient flowing streamers stand defiant, bringing a splash of colour to the garden for about three weeks at the bleakest time of year. The grass-green leaves appear in mid-spring, and some varieties colour up well during the autumn.

The largest flowers of all witch hazels belong to the hybrids of *Hamamelis x intermedia*. This is a natural cross between the Chinese species, *H. mollis*, and the Japanese *H. japonica*. Hybrids only occurred when these two geographically separated species were placed side by side in arboreta. Today, there are lots of named varieties, many of them deliberately bred. Because there's so much variety, and so much confusion regarding names, you should buy witch hazels in flower so you can see what you're getting. Also, consider the shape of the shrub. Look for a well-balanced, branching framework of outward-stretching branches.

Some witch hazels are more fragrant than others. The strongest, sweetest fragrance belongs to *Hamamelis x intermedia* 'Pallida', a sulphur-yellow witch hazel first discovered at RHS Wisley in 1958. These pallid yellow flowers, which stand out well against drab winter skies, smell strongly of freesias. I also grow another freesia-scented witch hazel called 'Aurora'. This is one of the best, with very large, peachy-orange flowers, reminiscent of the colour of fleshy butternut squash, borne in midwinter. A warm, still afternoon will release the pungent perfume of both of these witch hazels, and you could pick a branch or two to bring fragrance into the house.

The bright golden yellows include the later-flowering, pleasantly scented *Hamamelis x intermedia* 'Arnold Promise', which will also give you good autumn leaf, and 'Barmstedt Gold', an upright witch hazel with long, golden ribbons held against dark calices. Most of the yellows have a mixed spice fragrance somewhere between cinnamon and musk. However, not all witch hazels are as scented. 'Jelena' is a warm brown-orange with no scent at all, and the wide-spreading 'Diane' only produces a little scent from her cheery red flowers that cling to the whole length of the stem.

Many gardeners seem reluctant to try witch hazels, possibly because they are relatively costly, but they should do well provided they're given a humus-rich soil, with a pH of between 4.5 and 6.5. (Sequestered iron can be added to remedy chlorotic plants on limy or chalky soil.) When planting, make sure you allow plenty of space around your witch hazel. This not only looks better, but it also allows the summer sun to reach the wood more easily so it can produce more flower buds. Witch hazels in deep shade set few or no flowers. Sometimes a dull summer can spoil the bud set, but conversely a sunny summer will produce an abundance of flower six months hence. I have also found that my witch hazels, grown on limy soil, have a biennial tendency, flowering well in alternate years.

Placing witch hazels where the sun reaches the branches does create a gardening dilemma, for all like cool moisture at their roots in summer (this is a trait of many Chinese and Japanese plants). Water them well in dry summers by gently pouring over buckets of water, or leaving a gentle hose on them overnight. As with all plants, thorough watering sends the root system downwards, while ineffective watering, sprinkling them with a hose for a few minutes, will encourage surface roots and will make the situation worse. When summer conditions become too dry, a witch hazel will angle its leaves sharply downwards until they are vertical in a natural attempt to avoid transpiration. This is a distress flare, and should prompt you into giving it a long drink. Although it generally survives drought well, you will be rewarded with a much better crop of winter flowers if you keep it well watered in dry periods. This need for summer moisture is balanced by a need for good winter drainage. Digging airy, friable compost into the soil when you plant will help.

Once your witch hazel is established, you can tip the long branches back and shorten the laterals in late spring. This will help to produce more flowers as well as prevent it from romping away.

Other yellows

One of the great sights of winter is *Cornus mas*, commonly called the Cornelian cherry, a small tree that reaches 5m (15ft) high. It bears small bundles of clear yellow flowers on the end of the branches, and although as individuals they are much less spectacular than the witch hazel, the round clusters of yellow flowers stand out dramatically against a blue sky. The Cornelian cherry has impeccable timing, as it is always at its peak just as the snowdrops open. There are different forms of this hardy, easy-to-grow tree. *C. mas* 'Aurea' has bright yellow young leaves that age to green, 'Variegata' is a clean green leaf with a white margin, and 'Golden Glory' is a fine selection that bears red cherries in autumn, but only after a hot, sunny summer.

If your garden is in a warm, sheltered site, where summers are mild and damp – perhaps it enjoys a maritime climate – you may be able to encourage the Chinese *Edgeworthia chrysantha* into flower. This fragrant plant is on my 'must attempt' list, and whenever I see it producing its yellow flowers backed in white-silk cobweb hairs, I feel a touch of envy, for this oriental is unlikely to tolerate the hot, dry summers inflicted on my Cotswold garden.

The pale primrose-yellow flowers of corylopsis are more obliging, and garden centres are full of young plants dripping with long catkins of tiny, cup-shaped flowers that smell of sweet cowslips. There is some confusion over the naming of plants in this small genus of seven species that hail from China, Japan or the Himalayas. The earliest to flower is *Corylopsis pauciflora*, a plant that has masses of midwinter flowers made up from short tassels of two to three flowers. 'Pauciflora' literally means 'few flowers', and refers to the number of flowers in each individual tassel rather than the number of tassels, which cover the tree each year. There is also another corylopsis, *C. sinensis* var. *sinensis* (often mistakenly labelled *C. pauciflora*), with long tassels of flowers from early to mid-spring.

When visiting garden centres and nurseries early in the year, you may well see another plant bearing pale yellow tassels, *Stachyurus praecox*. These racemes are much longer and stiffer than corylopsis, and there are usually four or five tassels, each containing between 15 and 24 flowers, hanging in a row from the bare branches. This Japanese shrub reaches 2–3m (6–10ft) high.

Both corylopsis and stachyurus need sheltered sites to protect their flowers, as cold spring winds will cause the branches to die back. The ideal site is under the canopy of a deciduous tree. The pale flowers can be underplanted with small blue bulbs – the accommodating *Scilla sibirica* would be my choice, especially with the long-tasselled corylopsis. Pruning of corylopsis and stachyurus is always kept to a minimum, just a straight tidy, removing dead, diseased or dying tips after flowering.

LEFT *Growing Edgeworthia chrysantha is a challenge. To do well it needs a sheltered site away from wind, but it has a heavenly scent and is worth the battle.*

Cream and butterscotch flowers

Chinese, non-climbing honeysuckles can be grown in any garden, and all bear midwinter, downward-facing cream flowers that are sweetly scented. The Scottish plant hunter Robert Fortune collected two similar forms from China in 1845, the cream-flowered *Lonicera fragrantissima* and the white-with-a-hint-of-pink *L. standishii*. The hybrid between the two is the one you should grow, *L.* x *purpusii*. It bears cream flowers, and there is a very floriferous form called *L.* x *purpusii* 'Winter Beauty,' raised by Hillier Nurseries. 'Winter Beauty' begins flowering on almost bare wood in late winter, but ekes out its flowers until spring, when the first leaves begin to break. The cream flowers have a honeysuckle fragrance and make excellent cut flowers. The price you pay is that this twiggy bush can look untidy in leaf. I think it's worth it though, and have always stationed these honeysuckles close to gates, paths and seats,

ABOVE *Lonicera x purpusii 'Winter Beauty' is obligingly easy and the perfect winter-flowering shrub for a gateway.*

where their fragrance can be enjoyed at close quarters as you pass by.

Wintersweet, or *Chimonanthus praecox*, is another fragrant Chinese shrub with pale flowers. It needs a frost-free spot in the garden – a sun-baked wall would be ideal. This large shrub will grow up to 3m (10ft) tall and only flowers after about five years, so patience is vital. The pale, waxy blooms, which have purple centres, have a butterscotch colouring I like, and I can remember vases of these transparent beauties scenting a room in my childhood. There is also a pale yellow form I admire called 'Luteus'.

After flowering, the long whips are trimmed back to encourage new growth, and sun is then needed to ripen the wood. All too often, British summers fail to do the job well enough. This, combined with our habit of impulse-buying plants in full flower from the garden centre bench, doesn't favour the wintersweet, which only flowers when several years old, so it's becoming harder to find.

Warm pinks

Pale pink blossom, whether on a shrub or tree, brings a lovely, soft, warm glow to the garden, making winter actually seem warmer. Tone it with some plummy hellebores, or pink-red bergenias to enhance the effect. There are two main sources of pale pink in the garden at this time of year: the early viburnums, and the superb winter-flowering cherry *Prunus subhirtella* 'Autumnalis'.

SCENTED EARLY VIBURNUMS Viburnums are indispensable in the winter garden. Several deciduous varieties provide flowers in midwinter, and there are also one or two evergreens and semi-evergreens that flower a little later. The smaller-headed viburnums are particularly charming. They preside more happily over early flowers and bulbs without dominating them, unlike some of the more heavy-headed, globular forms. The flowers of early viburnums are not indestructible – heavy frosts can cause them to turn brown, postponing the show until later.

Viburnum x bodnantense 'Dawn' was bred at Bodnant around 1935 by Lord Aberconway's head gardener, F.C. Puddle. Bodnant enjoys a mellow climate on the banks of the River Conwy in North Wales, and it's a superb garden to visit. We must be thankful that it has given us 'Dawn', one of the finest winter-flowering shrubs available to the gardener. This tall, upright shrub can reach 3m (10ft) high, and is therefore best grown at the back of a woodland border, on a boundary, or as a specimen in a lawn. The hyacinth

fragrance with vanilla overtones is so strong, particularly in the dank days of late autumn, that it can pervade the whole garden regardless of where you place it. The flowers of 'Dawn' are a strong almond-pink, and they begin to appear when the old leaves are still on the shrub in late autumn. Then, as the leaves drop, they keep going on bare wood. By the time the new leaves appear in mid-spring, the last of the flowers are opening. They manage to flower for months, because of their stop-start habit of shutting down when the temperature drops and then carrying on again when it rises.

Viburnum x *bodnantense* 'Deben', bred in Suffolk, is a paler, more compact form, with pale pink buds opening to white. It is equally scented and just as floriferous, and its compact size (usually reaching only 2m/6ft high), should earn it a place in more gardens.

Both *bodnantense* hybrids are a cross between two species, *Viburnum grandiflorum* and *V. farreri*. *V. grandiflorum* has a sturdier habit, but doesn't do well in the garden and can be later-flowering. However, the erect *V. farreri* (formerly known as *V. fragrans*) flowers from late autumn to late winter, and produces long, slender stems each topped with a cluster of pink buds that open to produce white flowers. The pure-white form *V. farreri* 'Candidissimum' is one of the loveliest winter shrubs, and the bright green leaves are an added bonus. Both are more compact and tidier than 'Dawn' and 'Deben', and they have a sweeter scent. In mild winters, *V. x burkwoodii* may flower too. It has dark, glossy leaves, which remain through winter, and flatter heads of flowers, reminiscent of one of its parents, *V. carlesii*. It cannot be relied upon though, and is far more likely to give you a display in mid-spring than winter.

In recent years, some of my viburnums have died suddenly, in flower one week and gone the next. I haven't been able to throw much light on the problem, but it is something you should be aware of, as other gardening friends have reported the same thing.

PINK-TINGED WINTER-FLOWERING CHERRY

Prunus x subhirtella 'Autumnalis' is a delightful cherry for the winter garden, and if there's one flowering tree to find room for in your winter Eden, this is it. While so many flowers look drab against grey skies, this light, airy tree – with its tiny, pink-tinged white flowers set against dark, knobbly stems – shines and glimmers on even the dullest of days.

Despite its name, this tends to be a winter- rather than an autumn-flowering tree. Blossom on the sheltered side will open gradually in midwinter – just a few flowers to start with, as a light aperitif before the main course. Then, as winter really deepens, more tiny blush-pink flowers will open until all the branches are spangled in specks of pale blossom. Petals will drop in strong winds, like small snowflakes in the breeze, scudding along the ground as they go; I used to chase them along the school playground as a child on bitter winter days. The fragile flowers of this winter beauty are considerably more delicate than those of spring cherries.

There is a shell-pink form, *Prunus x subhirtella* 'Autumnalis Rosea', which is the same size as the pink-tinged white variety, about 8m (25ft) high. However, it isn't as stunning, as it doesn't display the same striking contrast of light blossom set against dark branches. There are also several other named forms on offer, including doubles and weeping cherries.

RIGHT *Delicate pale flowers on a dark, airy tree sum up this winter-flowering cherry –* Prunus x subhirtella *'Autumnalis'.*

Flowers set on bare branches are a great delight in winter, but there are also some evergreen plants that flower. They are great comforters of the soul, providing both foliage and blooms simultaneously.

flower set against leaf

Daphnes are a winter essential. If you're thinking of planting a daphne, opt for a form of the easy-to-grow evergreen *Daphne odora*, which will flower from late winter to early spring in sheltered, milder areas. 'Aureomarginata' is more reliable, hardier and more flower-packed than the plain species. It will form a wide mound, sometimes reaching 1.5m (5ft), although mine has never managed to reach more than 1m (3ft). The green leaves of 'Aureomarginata' are very faintly edged in yellow-cream and are subtle enough not to jar against the pink flowers. Choose a sheltered position, which gets some sun during winter, and somewhere in the garden that you pass by or visit frequently, where you can enjoy the scent.

The columnar *Daphne bholua* 'Jacqueline Postill', raised in 1982 by Alan Postill of Hillier Nurseries and named after his wife, outperforms all other winter-flowering evergreens. It has warm green leaves and waxy, mauve-pink flowers in mid-winter, and the heady, intoxicating fragrance wafts through the garden on still afternoons. 'Jacqueline Postill' is special in several ways. It flowers when in full leaf, whereas most other forms of *D. bholua* produce flowers on bare or sparsely leaved wood. It also has larger flowers, with slightly backward-arching petals. All *D. bholuas* reach 2m (6ft).

The evergreen 'Jacqueline Postill' won't be as tough as the deciduous, white-flowered *Daphne bholua* var. *glacialis* 'Gurkha' or the pink-budded, white-flowered *D. bholua* 'Darjeeling', because the deciduous forms grow at a higher altitude than the evergreens in their own wild habitats, so they are

BELOW The best flowering winter evergreen of all is the sumptuously fragrant Daphne bholua 'Jacqueline Postill'.

ABOVE *Smaller and more frost-tolerant than the species,* Daphne laureola subsp. philippi *has pretty clusters of pale greenish yellow blooms framed by whorls of shiny dark green leaves in late winter.*

used to colder temperatures. This means that if your garden is in a cold or exposed site, you may be restricted to the hardier deciduous forms, unless you can find some shelter from a west wall or an overhead tree. In my garden, the temperatures plummet in winter, but 'Jacqueline Postill' has still been a huge success, tucked safely under the benign canopy of the old apple tree among my hellebores and snowdrops.

So if you find a good sheltered location, yours should thrive too.

The yellow flowers of *Daphne jezoensis*, a small prostrate Japanese species, appear from late autumn through winter. In summer, this daphne drops every leaf, but it is only resting (I wonder how many gardeners have written it off as a disaster?). There is also another prostrate, cream-flowered daphne called *D. blagayana*, which is sometimes evergreen in mild climates and supposed to flower in late winter, although I haven't had much luck. Both species need a cool root run and prefer acid soil. I have taken to growing them in containers of ericaceous compost, placing them where they get late morning sun.

Although daphnes generally make wonderful garden plants, they do seem to have a death wish. When I meet up with friends in late winter, there are always one or two who start their conversations with a sad tale of their daphne's demise – it cuts across the whole range of them. Whenever you have a daphne that is doing really well, soften the blow and plant another as an insurance against the inevitable. They may wane slowly, becoming sparse of leaf and yellowing like a jaundiced man, or may collapse all of a sudden, in full regalia – I'm not sure which is worse.

Shade-loving mahonias

As houses become more closely thronged, many gardens are cast into deep shade. This causes difficulties for most winter-flowering shrubs, as they tend to prefer sun and warmth. However, the tall, upright mahonias, which fountain upwards to a height of 2.5m (8ft) or more to produce a crown of flower from the very top of the branches, are perfect for this position. These upright mahonias originate in eastern Asia, especially China, and are very different from the lower-growing, spreading American mahonias known as the Oregon grapes (*Mahonia aquifolium*). You often see the latter in municipal plantings, with their reddish leaves, yellow spring flowers, and black autumn berries, and they are considerably less attractive than their oriental, winter-flowering counterparts.

Mahonias are members of the Berberidaceae, and they are an example of those plants that became divided into oriental and occidental when the continents drifted apart thousands of years ago. The Japanese leatherleaf, or *Mahonia japonica* (which is actually from China and probably Taiwan) flowers

BELOW *Scented racemes of bright yellow flowers top the hybrid* Mahonia x *'Charity'; avoid planting* Mahonia aquifolium – *a scruffy shrub.*

in winter, producing arching, lemon-yellow flower spikes 30cm (12in) long. It is adept at performing in deep shade, and will also provide the gardener with good red leaf colour in autumn.

The finest mahonia is often considered to be *Mahonia lomariifolia*, a species from Yunnan, southwest China, first introduced to Britain by Major Johnson, owner of Hidcote Manor, Gloucestershire, in 1931. It has an open habit and long leaves consisting of up to 20 pairs of bright green leaflets. The clusters of long, rich yellow flower spikes appear in mid-autumn through to late winter. Although *M. lomariifolia* is one of the least hardy mahonias, surviving only in very mild positions, some of the best early-flowering forms are derived from it. These include *M.* x *media* 'Charity' (probably a hybrid crossed with the hardier *M. japonica*). It has good green foliage, long-flowering, warm yellow panicles, and is fully hardy. *M.* x *media* 'Winter Sun' has elegant foliage and more erect flowers, and 'Arthur Menzies' has lemon-yellow flowers. All will produce fragrant flowers in winter.

Fragrant evergreens

Certain plants announce their presence by their scent, and often these have tiny flowers that take some finding.

RIGHT The pink and cream flowers of Sarcococca hookeriana var. digyna *are the most heavily scented of all Christmas box varieties, but it doesn't have the purity of* S. confusa.

In recent years, Christmas box, or sarcococca, has increased in popularity. These are small evergreens that, at first glance, could be mistaken for box (*Buxus sempervirens*). The flowers are mere collections of stamens, but they are highly fragrant. I can remember being stunned by the heady scent of *Sarcococca confusa* at the Ness Botanic Gardens near Chester. I couldn't understand where the lily-like fragrance was coming from until, finally, I pinned it down to a small, compact plant, 30cm (12in) high. Needless to say, I rushed off to buy one. *S. confusa* is one of the finest winter-flowering scented plants, combining fresh green leaves and pure ivory-white flowers. The best examples I've ever seen grow at Cranborne Manor in Dorset, on the sides of the winterbourne. The whole area floods in winter but dries out in summer, and *S. confusa* has thrived, forming large bushes all along the streamside. Copious moisture seems to be a requirement of sarcococca. Conversely, in my own dry garden, *S. confusa* hasn't done well. It virtually stood still and lost leaf in summer. As a result, I've had to content myself by growing it in containers, close to doorways, where it performs well and produces lots of flower followed by a crop of black berries.

There are other species of sarcococca that are even more scented, but not quite as elegantly lovely to look at as *Sarcococca confusa. S. hookeriana* var. *digyna* has the most heavily scented flowers of all, yet they are a dingier combination of cream and red stamens, and the narrow, more leathery leaves are slightly yellowing in tone. *S. orientalis* has pink-stamened flowers and also lacks the beauty of *S. confusa*. However, whatever the species, tucking several sarcococca around the garden in containers will give great pleasure, and whenever the temperatures rise the smell of lilies will pervade.

One other plant with tiny flowers, *Azara microphylla,* also announces its presence by its scent. I first came across it in Terry Dagley's Worcestershire garden, where I came through a hedge and reeled at the aroma of pure vanilla essence – but where did it spring from? A tall, rangy small tree with shiny leaves arranged on herringbone twigs greeted me, but the tiny clusters of yellow flowers, again made from collections of stamens, were almost hidden away under the stems. *A. microphylla* is the hardiest of all the azaras, which hail from Chile or Argentina. Terry has managed to grow it in the garden, under the shelter of trees, and I have tucked it away on a south-facing wall. There is also a variegated form, with pink and cream leaves, and this looks lighter and prettier than the plain green form in summer.

Camellias: a moveable feast

Many camellias produce showy winter flowers against bold, glossy evergreen leaves, but they are acid-loving plants that turn up their toes on the neutral to alkaline soil moist of us have. However, I get great pleasure from growing camellias in containers. If you buy a good form when the plant is still small, and use ericaceous compost, camellias in pots will grow away and produce fat buds full of promise in no time at all. If the weather is dry in spring, you will have to water them, preferably using water from a butt rather than tap water in limy areas.

My favourite camellia for a container is a named hybrid of *Camellia* x *williamsii*. The original cross was made by J.C. Williams of Caerhays Castle, west Cornwall, in 1925 and was between *C. japonica* and *C. salvenensis*, and there are now many named forms. These hybrids are able to form buds in lower temperatures than other camellias, and they can flower freely from late autumn until late spring. Most come in shades of pink, and their flower shape varies between almost single to peony-flowered double. Forms include *C.* x *williamsii* 'Donation', a semi-double orchid pink; 'Debbie', which is a more stridently pink flounced double; the full-petalled, double rose-pink 'Joan Trehane', and the single, soft-almond-pink 'Winton'.

The problem with camellias – as with all acid-loving understorey plants such as azaleas, rhododendrons and magnolias – is that as soon as the frost touches the petals the flower browns. In fact, it isn't the frost that does the

RIGHT *Varieties of* Camellia x williamsii *are easy to grow and drop their spent flowers – while other camellias tend to cling to their dead.*

damage, it's the quick thaw caused by early morning sunlight. The advantage with putting these plants in pots is you can place the plant away from morning and midday sun, hopefully avoiding serious browning. A west wall is the best protection, and a north wall can also work well, as long as your house is not exposed to extreme northerlies too often.

Always choose a large, thick pot made from frost-proof terracotta, to prevent the roots from freezing over the winter. If bud set is poor, move your pot into a warm place during summer to ripen the wood. Once the bud is set, move it to a sheltered site where it will get only afternoon sun. You may have to invest in a trolley with wheels to accomplish this freedom of movement, but it will be worth it.

A sunny wall is a valuable asset, especially in winter. If you're lucky enough to have one, it is well worth planting one of the winter-flowering clematis bred from *Clematis cirrhosa*, a pale bell-flowered species from southern Europe.

walls of flower

The fern-leaved form of *Clematis cirrhosa* – var. *balearica* – is my favourite. It flowers in late winter, sometimes earlier, and produces pendant, cream-yellow flowers, spotted in maroon-red, set against dark green ferny leaves. After the flowers fade, tiny, fluffy heads appear and last through summer. As late summer arrives, this plant has a rest, looking dead and leafless for at least two months, but it springs back in late autumn or early winter.

It does have a habit of travelling upwards, framing doors and windows and creeping into the eaves if you have a bungalow. But you have to look up into pendant, overhead flowers to appreciate them in any case, so this isn't a problem. Their habit of setting seed has produced several forms. One of them, *C. cirrhosa* var. *purpurascens* 'Freckles', will give you even earlier flowers, producing its heavily red-spotted, larger cream bells by late autumn. There are other forms too, including the all-cream *C. cirrhosa* 'Wisley Cream' and the paler *C. cirrhosa* var. *purpurascens* 'Jingle Bells'.

The same wall could also support a spring-flowering *Clematis armandii*. The sweetly scented flowers will not open until mid-spring, but the clusters of plump, light green buds set against

LEFT *The ferny dark leaves of* Clematis cirrhosa var. balearica *show up the gently spotted cream flowers of this winter-flowering clematis.*

the long, leathery leaves and tendrils make a handsome winter feature in their own right. Another good reason for combining C. armandii with C. cirrhosa is that the former, although vigorous, can be tamed and kept low to clothe the wall, while the flowers of the latter scale the heights, thus providing a spectacular display at different levels. Pruning of winter-flowering cirrhosa clematis is always light, just a tidy after flowering.

I also like the evergreen Chilean shrub, Drimys winteri for the same reason as Clematis armandii: its fat buds and leathery green foliage cheer me in winter and it's another candidate for that sun-baked wall. Commonly called winter's bark, Drimys winteri hails from Chile, Mexico and Argentina, and it produces clusters of about 20 fragrant white, starry flowers in late spring. The bark is also aromatic on mature specimens. It can reach 15m (50ft) in height, but usually forms a wide bush some 3m (10ft) across.

index

Page numbers in *italics* refer to picture captions

Picture Credits

Val Bourne 41 bottom left, 47 top, 53 bottom centre, 117 centre left, 125 centre right top.

The Garden Collection /Barnsley House, Glos. 64 main picture; /Jonathan Buckley 4-5 main; /Liz Eddison 108 bottom; /Andrew Lawson 82-83 main picture; /Designer: Helen Yemm 42 bottom.

Garden Picture Library 36 bottom; /Anne Green-Armytage 54 bottom right, 127 top left; /Pernilla Bergdahl 153 main; /Richard Bloom 7 bottom; /Werner Bollmann 131 top centre left; /Mark Bolton 2-3 main picture, 29 top, 32-33 main picture, 110 bottom left, 133 bottom left, 67 top; /Chris Burrows 71 bottom left, 154 bottom left; /Brian Carter 87 top; /Eric Crichton 74 top left; /Claire Davies 120 top left; /Ron Evans 60 bottom right; /Berndt Fischer 112-113 main picture; /John Glover 28 bottom left, 69 top centre left, 89 bottom, 123 top, 124 bottom right, 129 bottom, 141 top centre right, 151 bottom centre right; /Sunniva Harte 135 bottom; /Jacqui Hurst 149 top; /Anne Hyde 14 top centre, 85 main picture; /Index Stock Imagery 86 bottom right; /Hernamt Jariwala 147 bottom right; /Lynn Keddie 142 top left; /Geoff Kidd 59 main; /A.I. Lord 81 main; /Susie McCaffrey 150 bottom; /Clive Nichols 93 bottom centre right, 132; /Jerry Pavia 90 top; /Brigitte & Philippe Perdereau 66 bottom centre; /Howard Rice 11 bottom, 22 bottom left, 35 main, 44 main, 70 top left, 78 top right, 91 bottom left, 92 main picture, 94 bottom right, 115 main picture, 121 bottom, 122 bottom centre right, 126 bottom centre left, 130 bottom right, 136 bottom right, 140 bottom right, 146 top centre left, 155 main; /Mayer Le Scanff 13 bottom centre; /J.S. Sira 25 bottom centre right, 26 bottom, 96 top right, 116 bottom centre left, 118 bottom right; /Friedrich Strauss 37 centre right; /Didier Willery 19 bottom left, 52 main, 95 bottom centre right; /Mark Winwood 50 bottom right.

Garden World Images /I. Anderson 43 top right.

Marianne Majerus 30 bottom right, 128 centre left, 137 top, 138-139 main picture.

Clive Nichols 6 top left, 8-9 main, 15 centre right, 16 top right, 17 bottom, 20 bottom left, 24 main picture, 31 top, 46 bottom centre, 61 top centre, 63 bottom, 73 bottom left, 76 bottom centre, 77 top, 119 top left, 134 centre left, 143 bottom centre left, 144 centre left, 145 top left, 148 bottom right; /Arrow Cottage Garden 100 centre left; /Val Bourne's Garden 40 top left; /Hazelbury Manor, Wilts. 98-99 main picture; /Lady Farm, Somerset 22-23 main picture; /John Massey 12 top right, 102 top centre left, 103 bottom left, 105 top, 106 bottom right, 107 top; /Clare Matthews 38 bottom centre left, 104 bottom centre right; /The Old Vicarage, Norfolk 51 top; /Oxford Botanical Gardens 109 top centre right; /Packwood House, Warwickshire 68 bottom; /Pettifers, Oxfordshire 1 top centre, 48 centre left, 49 bottom centre right, 101 top; /West Green House, Hampshire 34 bottom left, 56-57 main picture; /Woodchippings, Northants. 114 centre left.

Octopus Publishing Group Limited /Andrew Lawson 58 bottom left, 62 top right, 79, 84 top left, 75 bottom.

Author's Acknowledgements

A huge thank you to my editor Polly Boyd for her gentle touch, to Anna Cheifetz of Cassell for making this book happen so smoothly, and to Aruna Mathur and Austin Taylor for an inspirational layout. I'd also like to thank the many nursery and garden owners who've shared their knowledge so generously over the years, particularly Robert Vernon of the Bluebell Nursery in Leicestershire (for his generous help and advice about trees) and Paul Whittaker of PW Plants in Norfolk (for his expert advice on bamboo).

First published in Great Britain in 2006 by Cassell Illustrated, a division of Octopus Publishing Group Limited 2-4 Heron Quays, London E14 4JP

Text copyright © Val Bourne
Design and layout © Cassell Illustrated

The moral right of Val Bourne to be identified as the author of this Work has been asserted in accordance with the Copyright, Designs and Patents Act of 1988.

Distributed in the United States of America by Sterling Publishing Co., Inc., 387 Park Avenue South, New York, NY 10016-8810

A CIP catalogue record for this book is available from the British Library.

ISBN-13: 978-1-844034-81-9
ISBN-10: 1-844034-81-X

10 9 8 7 6 5 4 3 2 1
10 9 8 7 6 5 4 3 2 1

Printed in China

Designed by Austin Taylor
Edited by Polly Boyd
Publishing Manager Anna Cheifetz
Picture Researcher Aruna Mathur